STEPS OF COURAGE AND
KINDNESS TOWARD
JOYFUL LIVING

Father, May I...

Marjorie Wright Hawkins

outskirts
press

Father, May I...
Lessons from the Old-Fashioned Game of "Mother, May I," calling for Giant Steps of Courage and Kindness Toward Joyful Living

All Rights Reserved.
Copyright © 2022 Marjorie Wright Hawkins
v5.0

The opinions expressed in this manuscript are solely the opinions of the author and do not represent the opinions or thoughts of the publisher. The author has represented and warranted full ownership and/or legal right to publish all the materials in this book.

This book may not be reproduced, transmitted, or stored in whole or in part by any means, including graphic, electronic, or mechanical without the express written consent of the publisher except in the case of brief quotations embodied in critical articles and reviews.

Outskirts Press, Inc.
http://www.outskirtspress.com

ISBN: 978-1-9772-5064-3

Cover Photo © 2022 www.gettyimages.com. All rights reserved - used with permission.

Outskirts Press and the "OP" logo are trademarks belonging to Outskirts Press, Inc.

PRINTED IN THE UNITED STATES OF AMERICA

[The Human Touch]

All children need a laptop.
Not a computer, but a human laptop.
Moms, Dads, Grannies and Grandpas, Aunts, Uncles—someone to
    hold them, read to them, teach them.
Loved ones who will embrace them and pass on the experience,
    rituals and knowledge of a hundred previous generations.
Loved ones who will pass to the next generation their expectations
    of them, their hopes and their dreams.

Colin Powell

Acknowledgments

To nine enthusiastic, thoughtful, interactive grandchildren, who have blessed my journey with hours and hours of lap time, I dedicate this book. Ethan, Eli, Isabella, Elizabeth, John, Andrew, Lucia, Hannah and Thomas are precious gifts, genuinely grateful for the opportunity to grow up together. They have yet to forego a chance to support, communicate and spend fun times with each other.

For the extraordinary gifts of my husband, children, grandchildren, family and friends, my love, gratitude and hope for the future is unmeasurable. Thank you for the inspiration of Barb and Lois, who continue to grace my life. My heart is full.

An enormous thank you is showered upon a lifetime of teachers, both inside and outside the classroom. A special note of thanks to my winter writing group, "Compose Yourself." The sincere dedication and interest of educators, friends and family members, has planted energizing seeds of inspiration.

A heartfelt thank you comes with a lengthy embrace for my treasured sister, Patricia. At this wobbly stage of our lives, Patti challenged me to "fish or cut bait" on reeling in memories, and writing them down for others' enjoyment. She inspired my dive into a sea of scrapbooks and memory boxes and a great deal of "fishing around" in a mind growing softer. Her encouragement directed me in the task of casting meaning upon this "dubious" stage of life. The "catch of the day" became a goal that led me to tackle a book filled with events and memories, with the hope of restoring kindness and growing resilient in a world of "troubled waters." In the Gospel of John, Jesus miraculously fed thousands of people with 7 loaves of bread and two fish.

I couldn't resist my sister's confident lure, "you have a message of kindness to share." Perhaps, through the multiplication of good deeds in a world hungry for peace, harmony and freedom, thousands or millions can be nourished.

Table of Contents

Introduction i

The Way We Were 1
   Peeps, Pigs and Perseverance 3
   Field of Beans 6
   Good Ol' Days 8
   Down and Dirty 11
   Sentimental Journey 15
   School Days 20
   The Meeting Will Come to Order 24
   There's a Hole in the Bucket 28
   Reap What You Sow 32

Wipe Away Every Tear 35
   Trust on the Caring Bridge 37
   Angels Among Us 41
   The Greatest Things You'll Ever Know 46

We Are The Champions 55
   Ordinary Olympians 57
   "Do What You Love, Love What You Do" 60
   Happily Ever After 63
   I Pledge My Head… 66

Here Comes the Sun 71
   I Can See Clearly Now 73
   Marriage#Trust 76
   Deceased Diva 82
   Hello? 85

The "Good" in "Good-Bye" 87
Through the Years…with Brothers 90
Through the Years… with Sisters 94

Don't Stop Believing **99**
Jesus at Michael's 101
Flower Whisperer 104
Lookin' for Love in all the Wrong Places.............................. 106
Heroes In a Box 115
Keep a Song in Your Heart 118
No Scars.. 124
Rescued... 126

Ain't No Mountain High Enough.. **129**
Chicken Little's Warning 131
Sometimes You Win, Sometimes You Learn 135
More to the Story 138
Letter to My Younger Self 143
Giving Thanks... 146
I'm Gonna' Climb that Mountain 150
Epilogue 155

Introduction

AS AUGUST 31ST made its appearance on the calendar, I found myself shouldering a "boatload" of stress! Disbelief, fear and sadness were consuming bigger chunks of my thoughts and feelings!! So, with my sister's encouragement and my husband's support, I dialed my heart to "refocus!" God set the stage for a year of thoughtful journaling with His words in Psalms 139..."*O Lord, you have examined my heart and know everything about me...You chart the path ahead of me and tell me where to stop and rest. I can never be lost to your Spirit...your hand will guide me, your strength will support me. Thank you for making me so wonderfully complex. You saw me before I was born and scheduled each day of my life before I began to breathe. How precious it is, Lord, to realize that you are thinking about me constantly! Search me, O God, and know my heart; test my thoughts. Point out anything you find in me that makes You sad and lead me along the path of everlasting life.*"

The scary date has come and gone, and the 70th anniversary of the day I was born in the Paris Hospital is but a memory. During the first two weeks of September, 1943, Mom and I bonded during a typical stay in the Illinois hospital. Dad picked us up and wrote out a check to our family doctor for $25 dollars. Seventy years later, Minnesota lit up my birthday stage with 90 degree sunshine, a cloudless blue sky, an 80 degree sparkling lake, a loving husband, six thoughtful children and spouses and nine energetic grandchildren to squash the fear of reaching my 70th birthday.

Banishing thoughts of infirmity, wrinkles, aches and numbers, I quickly shifted gears throughout the week-end in sync with the delightful sounds, tastes, activities (including frog surgery and romps with our 4 legged family members, Bingo and Tori). On that particular birthday, we did not play "Mother, May I." But I do recall the laughter from my own childhood, when my siblings and neighborhood friends engaged in this outdoor game, asking politely for permission to follow the directions of "Mother." The Mother or Father, with back turned, called out a number of baby steps, giant steps, umbrella steps, frog hops, crabwalks, Cinderella steps, open and shut the book jumps or lamppost positions, moving players forward or backward. Players who forgot to ask, "Mother, (or Father, or Captain), may I?" were required to go back to the starting line.

Remembering those days, coupled with the current joy of engaging with grandchildren gave me every reason to take a stroll down Memory Lane. Real-life anecdotes and stories, along with inspirational Scripture and personal prayers, illustrating my own journey, fill the pages of this book. I wrote about life experiences, what I learned, how it contrasts with 21st century feelings and behaviors and how resolution might be inspired in the minds and hearts of God's children. Who knew the second half of my reflections would be recorded during a frightening, life-changing pandemic?

Perhaps, new steps will be added to the earthly game of "Mother, May I"....*Triple Booster Twirls, Jumping Jabs, Masked Monkey Moves, Fauci Flips or Covid* Circles. Nonetheless, everyone is a winner when guidance is sought and followed, asking faithfully, "Father, May I?"

The Way We Were

Peeps, Pigs and Perseverance

ONE DARK WINTER morning, when I was about ten years old, I was headed to the brooder house, toting a bucket of chicken feed for my 200 4-H baby chicks. On my way, all was quiet in the predawn as I approached the cozy little, softly lighted building. I stepped into the warm, pungent space and executed a terrified jump when an owl began to screech at the top of its lungs! I had not heard the owl screaming during the night when it flew toward the lights of the brooder house and got stuck in the wire mesh covering the outside of each window. I quickly realized that the window glass protected me from the owl, but as I focused on the baby chicks, my heart plummeted straight to the bottom of my gum boots. In the far corner, all of those tiny, little yellow fuzzy chicks were piled upon one another. In their fright, more that half of the baby chicks had died from suffocation as they tried to get away from the awful noise. I was DEVASTATED!

A decade later, during the 50's and 60's, my high school had a social club for girls. Only a small number of girls were invited to join the club each year and on the day that invitations were sent to the new invitees, tension was high! On the 30 minute bus ride home from high school that day, my best friend got off the bus, jerked open the mailbox and before the bus resumed its route down the road, Sharon was waving her invitation jubilantly. When I arrived home, I too, grabbed the mail from the mailbox, eagerly shuffled through the envelopes and other "mail," and thought 'surely there has been a mistake' when there was no invite addressed to Marjorie. I was crushed, devastated, and sooooo heartbroken! I "lost it" in the tearful crush of DISAPPOINTMENT!

Devastation and Disappointment ....at the moment...so hard to face....so hard to understand....and so hard to overcome. Neither Mom nor Dad jumped in to "fix" things (they couldn't afford more chicks; no way would they approach the high school club sponsors to insist that they had made a mistake)! And yet, they somehow instilled the message that I was strong enough to "move on," face another day, stand up to the struggle, overcome the heartache and persevere. And I did, because they believed in me. They didn't read a book about it and they didn't have a philosophy about it, but they nurtured the development of resilience and perhaps, most importantly, began building the skill to persevere when the challenges would become greater. Leaving home for Minnesota years later (when we were sure we had reached the end of the earth); dealing with unexpected job changes; and grieving the loss of grandparents, extended family members, long-time friends, children of close friends further shook our ability to persevere. Our inability to "fix" all of the struggles and heartaches encountered by our own children were invaluable lessons. While Dad's commands were clear, short and did not involve negotiation or lengthy explanation, Mom was gentle, reassuring, but also brief. "You will be fine...keep your chin up!" They, after all, had known the dual, ultimate despair of losing children through the devastating experiences of "giving away" a child and reeling from the "forever" heartbreak of their two-year-old child's death. So, how did they do that?? How did their children learn perseverance without them really "teaching" it?

I don't remember that they ever thought about or taught "perseverance," but I believe it flourished within unconditional "support," independent of what others might think. I can describe it by calling to mind an image created in the kitchen of the farmhouse where a brother, sister and I grew up. As very young children, we were exposed to the dangers that faced tiny baby pigs upon their birth. Either momma pig unknowingly rolled over on them shortly after birth, or the stronger pigs muscled the "runts" out of the way as they sought warm, life-sustaining milk. Each spring when our Hampshire and Poland China pigs gave birth to new piglets, there were invariably a few runts whose lives were compromised from the moment of birth. Mom and Dad struggled to keep them alive, feeding them whiskey-laced milk from a coke bottle with a long nipple, wrapping them in a towel and letting them sleep in a box in a warm oven (with the door open!). The runt piglets received the "support" they needed, not just to survive, but to "thrive" as they struggled against the challenges of being "under-developed, weak, insecure, and scared."

Those same challenges face all children during developmental years of uncertainty, when fear, disillusionment and attention seeking can so easily take center stage. Trials, heartaches, stumbling blocks and denied wishes are critical for healthy development of children. Working through the difficulty in hearing NO, facing challenges of not keeping up with the Joneses, disappointments, stumbles, childhood bullying and a hundred other "rough spots," is undeniably tough, but perseverance, starting at a very early age, with "you can handle this" is bound to pay off. The most devastating message we unwittingly plant in our children is…. "Let me show you how much I love you, by how much I give you and how easy I can make things for you. Perseverance gets lost when there are no obstacles to overcome.

Field of Beans

AS MY HUSBAND and I drive through the Minnesota countryside during the sunny, dry month of August, more often than not, we remark about "the pretty fields of beans!" That descriptor is earned in a field where the dark green rows curve around the hillside perfectly spaced, with no visible evidence of weeds. I remember the scorn, with which Mom and Dad viewed a field of "succotash," an ugly mixture of beans and last year's corn (now presenting as weeds).

Weeds were a big deal in Dad's farming frame of reference. He did not like them in the ditches along the road. He did not like them along the fence rows and he did not like them in the bean rows. One summer day, Dad took us to the bean field on the back corner of the farm. I am not sure if we were being punished, taught a lesson about the virtues of work or Dad was tired of hearing "I'm bored," but the next thing my siblings and I knew, we were standing at the end of very long rows of beans with random corn stalks popping up every so often. We were directed to "walk the rows," and pull out the "visible corn stalk" weeds. When we arrived at the other end, we were to select another set of rows and head back pulling out more corn stalks. In an "aha" moment, I shared a genius plan with my siblings that suggested we each take four rows at a time, criss-crossing the rows by jumping over them to "save steps" and get out of the July Illinois heat and humidity a lot faster. We started off with a head of steam and about half-way down the first row, our legs were BURNING! The pace slowed and I have blotted out any recollection of how this "work experience" ended, but I was very careful to consider whatever had provoked it in the first place. There surely was a lesson here and once again I am pushed to give credit to the exercise/boredom-buster/exercise genius of "Tai Chi U.G!"

About 600 years before Ulysses Grant (U.G/Dad) was born, in true Asian fashion, Chang San-feng, legendary founder of T'ai Chi Ch'uan, reflected upon the "weeds of the mind." San-feng declared that the fertile field cannot produce good crops as long as the weeds are not cleared away. Dad knew that from his own experience and decided to include that knowledge in our upbringing. San-feng went on to label cravings and vexations as "weeds of the mind" and if they, too, are not cleared away, concentration and wisdom do not develop. Was there wisdom emerging as our legs turned to jelly in our quest for a "pretty field?" I do know I concentrated on how to avoid getting that job ever again!!

Dad's philosophy was simply "hard work never hurt anyone." I'm dead sure, however, that Dad's perspective on "lessons learned" in his field of beans would not have pondered "weeds of the mind." Chang's message extended beyond weeds to acceptance, releasing the uncontrollable and learning to engage productively with the unpleasant. There's a life-changing message here! Instead of emphasizing each tiny weed in our cluttered minds or focusing angrily on last year's "sprouting upsets" in life's journey, my desire is to walk the positive walk and engage in positive talk, creating a kind "beauty" of life where we value and appreciate one another. Thinking about the weeds in my mind encourages me to consider alternative points of view in the big picture, although I am pretty sure Dad would still be doubting whether Mr. Tai Chi really knew "beans about beans!"

Good Ol' Days

I WONDER IF our children, who are now parents of our grandchildren, ever wish for the simplicity of their youth? Our childhood "fun" in the 40's and 50's almost exclusively focused on yard games, a couple of visits to the city lake or swimming pool each summer, throwing snowballs or building snow forts, seeing a Tom Mix movie or watching Mickey Mouse Club, a dash through the cornfield playing Cowboys and Indians and replays of Joey Chitwood's Auto Daredevils on our own bicycles and homemade ramps. Dolls and a basketball hoop (hooked to the backyard light pole), haymow tunnels, Monopoly, card games and hours of sandbox activities kept our recreation simple, inexpensive and healthy (mostly outside and active....strengthening bodies and practicing interactive skills).

John, Marjorie, Patricia at home

During those active days of our youth, if my siblings and I were bored, we didn't dare announce it...or Dad, especially, was always ready with a long list of "opportunities" to relieve that boredom. Usually, we created our own entertainment. When we had exhausted the usual activities, we came up with "more advanced" challenges, such as climbing onto the roof of the "cowshed/garage" via the lightning rod. The twisted wire rod was conveniently curved to facilitate our climb onto the roof....unseen by adults in the vicinity! We even supplied each other with umbrellas and jumped off of the roof "floating" very quickly to the ground.

In another burst of inspiration, my brother, playing Pirate (I guess), chased me with a butcher knife. He got his "ho-ho-ho-never-do-that-again" punishment from Dad when the knife was replaced with a tree branch, destined for his rear end. We also found front-row-seat entertainment sitting on top of the white wooden fence between our back yard and the feedlot as we cheered and applauded the unusual behavior of livestock jumping on the backs of other livestock. One evening, when Mom called "suppertime," her naive children yelled.... "we can't come now, we are watching a rodeo!" I don't remember the incident resulting in a heart-to-heart talk about reproduction....in fact, I don't recall any discussion during our childhood about sex. Mom's teaching was limited to conversation about a few drops of blood, the location of sanitary napkins in the bathroom cabinet, and the presentation of, "ugh".....an elastic sanitary belt! Those were not the good old days! I guess I figured out the sex part, thanks to Advanced Biology teacher, Mr. Waltman, his "crawl under the lab table" wall charts that had me cringing in my seat, and.....three beautiful children later.

There are few things I miss about the good old days. Cream pies, homemade ice cream, and less hectic days are on the list. I miss the comedic relief of Red Skelton, Jack Benny, Lucy and Tim Conway. I miss the entertaining variety shows of Bing Crosby, Bob Hope, Carol Burnett, Andy Williams and the Hit Parade. I miss the sitcoms of Mary Tyler Moore and Ozzie and Harriet. I miss Ed Sullivan and the Lennon

FATHER, MAY I...

Sisters, but those things are archived somewhere, if I want to hear them one more time. The things I can't access are family and friends who have completed their earthly journeys. I miss Mom and Dad and the good old days that underscored our family life.

I am so grateful when I hear parents making every effort to eat meals together and be genuinely present in their children's lives. In the fast-paced society we live in today, I am especially grateful for the ease of staying in touch through "in-the-moment" photos, texts and face-time. Connecting is easy and joyful...letting someone know you are thinking about them takes seconds. If I could have a "redo" on my youth, I would have been "more present" to the people I loved. There is just no greater gift than engaging intentionally and purposefully with people you love... yesterday, today and tomorrow. When the opportunity to engage more fully was lost, with Mom, Dad, my grandparents and other good people in my past, I grew a little wiser. I intend to feel the joy in positive engagement with those I love in all the "todays" I have left.

Children and adults today are seduced and challenged by 24-7 access to information and hard-to-leave entertainment. Are we losing the "wonder" of "wondering?" I am challenged to create "good ol' days" that my children and grandchildren will remember with a smile. I love creating in the kitchen; addressing weeds, sticks and mulch in the landscape; playing cards and dealing with place settings at the dining room table; creating art with rocks, cardboard and paint; creating "chore jars," building fairy houses, and enjoying campfire s'mores and stories. What's great about the "Good New Days" is the fact that I can still put forth effort to make a difference in the lives of my children, grandchildren, extended family and neighbors. Being present is my best guess to ensure our children and grandchildren will remember their "Good Ol' Days!"

Down and Dirty

AS THE END of September approaches, the trees are beginning to change color and there is a bit of a "nip" in the night air. With the flip of a switch, the gas fireplace lights up or a prescribed amount of heat floats through the grates. It's a Monday, and I might wash a load of "whites or colors." I might even mix the two together or wash one load today and another on Wednesday or Saturday. How our execution of laundry has changed in the last three-quarters of a century!

In the 1940's and 50's, heating the farm house and doing laundry involved tasks performed in our crude, concrete "full" basement. There was no cozy family room in that colorless, dimly lit area, but it was, nontheless, an important place for family activity. One basement room, near the enormous furnace, was filled regularly with coal which was shoveled into a burning fire inside the furnace, sending heat to the main floor of the house. (The heat did not reach the upper floor of bedrooms). I remember drawing burned "clinkers" out of the furnace with special tongs to cool and discard. I don't remember where the clinkers ended up. Later, one of my brother's tasks was to add coal to the "stoker," a truly modern invention that augered the coal automatically into the furnace so that the fire in the furnace burned more evenly and continually. Our favorite place during "heating" season was the large square grate in the dining room floor, where the warmth was heavenly!

The entire laundry process took place in the 1940's and 50's in our basement on Mondays where a wringer washer was engaged for several hours. One had to be extremely careful not to get an arm caught in the wringer that squeezed out excess water from the clothing. That did happen on more than one occasion! The whites were washed first, followed by the colors and finally, heavy, dirty work clothes that probably did not get washed every week. The same sequence was followed for family members in the galvanized tub next to the kitchen fire-fueled stove. Babies first...Dads last. The same laundry water was returned to the washing machine for subsequent loads thus the white to dark sequence. After all the clothes had been washed, the water was drained and a fresh load of water, dispensed with a hose, was used to rinse the three loads of clothes **for that week!** We wore the same pajamas all week and we changed to the same weekly play clothes when we arrived home from school. School clothes and Sunday clothes were washed only when needed.

Mom used homemade lye soap and a washboard to remove tough stains. For as long as the weather permitted, clothes were hung outside on the clotheslines to dry. Later, adjustable, aluminum pants hangers were slipped into pants and bluejeans, creating sharp creases in the pant legs. On cold days, the wet clothes froze while they were drying and were stiff as boards when we "took down" the clothes. If there was a lot of snow on the ground and the air was frigid, or it rained on Monday, clothes were hung on ropes crisscrossing the basement. Occasionally, clothes were dried on a wooden expandable rack near heat registers if Monday was a humid day and we were out of clean underwear. The only thing I miss about those laundry days is the sunshine fragrance of sheets and pillow cases that went straight from clothesline to bed. I plan to buy stock in the company that figures out how to bottle that wonderful, elusive smell of fresh air and sunshine.

In the back room of the basement stood a gray, decrepit old Pie Safe where Mom stashed garden vegetables with roots still attached and plenty of dirt to keep them fresh. At one point, Mom's brother, my Uncle Johnny carted the old off-balance, smelly "mouse residence" off to his workshop, where he straightened the boards, created new metal inserts with breathing holes and proceeded to rebuild and refinish the walnut cupboard. The refurbished Pie Safe became a work of art and for many years, stored Mom's white, silver trimmed Sunday dishes, along with her American Fostoria glassware, dessert plates and platters. Lennox Christmas serving dishes and sterling silver resided there too, along with hand painted china, created by her mother, Esther and grandmother Lillian. The beautiful Pie Safe, once destined to become firewood, resides safely in our home, holding memories of its functionality in both dining room and the initial "down and dirty" corner of the basement. Today it holds treasures of family gatherings and precious memories of what it takes to hold a family together.

When Dad was involved in very messy, dirty or smelly jobs involving animals or harvesting, he entered the house via the side porch and descended the wooden steps to the basement where a small shower head was perched in a corner of the basement ceiling for a quick shower. There was a drain, but no curtain (or glass wall) and we did not go to the basement when dad was removing the grime of a day's work.

On occasion, with heavy rains, the basement would flood, with sometimes 3 feet of water. The water was muddy and we relocated food and hanging clothes above the water, going barefoot or wearing gum boots. It usually took several days before the sour smelling water drained away and we swept up the remaining mud.

For years after I was married, I always washed the white clothes first even though each load had its own fresh water. Today, washers and dryers have ascended to the second story or multiple levels in new homes eliminating the need to carry clothes up and down steps. Furnaces and fireplaces require a flip of the switch or adjusting a thermostat to keep us toasty. Foods are available year-round in the local grocery store....or curbside...delivered to your front door any day of the week. Great Rooms encompass kitchens, dining and living areas, and have replaced family recreation rooms in lower levels. Furnaces are hidden in utility closets or storage rooms. Today's homes are often designed with an "inner safe room," replacing the need to camp out

FATHER, MAY I...

in a storm cellar during tornadoes. For what purpose, then, do we need a basement? I think Mom had the answer when she labeled steps up or down, her "Stairmaster!"

Sentimental Journey

THERE IS A small wooden sign hanging in our home that says "Grandparents....so easy to operate... a child can do it!" How we do love our grandchildren and want the best for them. Sometimes grandparents go down the wrong road making life too easy. Sometimes grandparents go down the wrong road by their lack of involvement in their grandchildren's lives. But I am convinced that all grandparents want the best for these precious children and I am sure my grandparents did too. Long after they have been gone, I realize what an amazing presence they had in the lives of myself, my siblings and cousins... and I don't think we small folk "operated" them at all.

Grandmother Wright Nichols figured dominantly in our lives from Day 1 (as well as before we were born). She always insisted that we call her Grandmother....no "gramma," or worse... "granny" for her! She was Determined (with a capital D) to make sure we were raised with values of strong work ethic, financial stability, appropriate manners, respect for elders, social skills, patriotism and no-nonsense behavior. It always seemed like my brother had priority attention— (new convertible, college tuition payments, family attendance at every sporting event). It was a surprise to me that Grandmother funded a large part of my college education when the canceled checks were shared with me long after graduation. Appearances were very important to Grandmother Wright and she made sure we had a few new, stylish clothes to wear. She hosted luncheons for girls my age, whom she deemed were good contacts. She bought corsages for all attendees at the luncheon; we used cloth napkins and practiced with appropriate silverware and conversation.

Florence Hale Wright Nichols. John, Marjorie, Patricia

SENTIMENTAL JOURNEY

Grandmother Wright lost her mother to mental illness at a vulnerable age and had to step up as mother-substitute. She lost her husband very early in a challenging marriage. She lost her son-in-law in his final days of military service during World War II. She lost control of her son, who deserted family values for a time, impregnating a young teen and ultimately running off to marry a minor. She lost their farm for a brief, but scary time. She lost her first grandchild at age two in a devastating accident with no penicillin to save this beautiful little girl.

All of these losses laid the foundation for a belief that Grandmother often shared... "you can love 'em rich as well as poor." I was more than a little disgruntled with this perspective. However, she practiced what she preached, and in midlife, married the owner of multiple successful Loan Offices. But this lovable guy, who looked just like Alfred Hitchcock, adored and appreciated my "bootstraps" Grandmother. How many husbands would come home every day for lunch and settle in the living room with their brides at precisely 12:30 p.m. each work day, delaying a return to the office for another hour while they laughed and cried "As The World Turned." I was pretty sure she felt safety for the first time in her life and I do believe she made her new husband very happy. The security was worth everything to her after a lifetime of losses. She relished the ability to provide for her family in ways that would have otherwise been impossible and to live without fear in the second half of her life. She was a great bridge player, loved to dance and grabbed whomever was closest to bounce along to the tunes of the 40's, 50's and 60's. Maybe my sister and I started their marriage off on the right note, when we sang "I'll Be With You In Apple Blossom Time" at their wedding in the south room of our farmhouse. "Happy the bride the sun [shined] on that day."

My Grandmother Wright Nichols gets well-deserved credit for two of the most important occurrences in my personal life. I was an eighth grader in the spring of 1957 when she sweetly "ordered" my brother and I to dress up and come with my grandparents to a youth dance in nearby Terre Haute, Indiana. My stepgrandfather was

FATHER, MAY I...

a member of the Terre Haute Country Club....and we didn't say "no" to Grandmother. I can still hear the click-click of the chaperone's high heels as she came across the slippery tile floor to the table where my 14 year old brother and I were sitting with our grandparents. With warm enthusiasm, she persuaded my brother and I to join her daughter's table of junior high friends near the pool deck. An immediate friendship was formed. My brother and I both enjoyed the subsequent, and long-lasting friendship of the chaperone's daughter, Susie. Eventually, after several sleep-overs, Susie insisted I meet her "across-the-alley" brother. A short time ago, that "brother" and I celebrated 55 years of marriage after a nine year courtship.

The second occurrence was my college education. Grandmother did not make a big deal or a big show about supporting my college expenses, but I graduated with a BS and MS without a cent of debt. How I regret my flippant remark during one Sunday dinner when my college days at Indiana State were history. Grandmother was suggesting that the best way to broil meat was to salt the meat before putting it under the broiler. I said, "no, you should salt the meat later because salt reduces the moistness of the meat as it cooks; after, all, Grandmother, I majored in Home Economics!" Oh my, "I am so sorry, Grandmother, for that arrogance.....after all that you sacrificed for me....not the least of which was that Home Ec major!"

On the opposite side of the coin, Grandaddy Gilbert was kind, gentle and a great Cub fan. I remember his quiet presence, never making waves about anything! He was present for most Sunday dinners and settled in the Laz-e-boy after dinner at noon for the Cubs games. He suffered losses, too, but kept them close to the vest. I only recently learned the story of his "life-changing" decision to accept Mom back into the family fold after she gave birth to a child out of wedlock and subsequently secretly married the baby's father...our Dad.

Grandaddy farmed all of his life and resided many years in the basement of his home with his son and family on the upper levels. As even those quarters grew too close for family harmony, he spent his final years in a room in a hotel in a nearby town. I remember being shocked at the sparse tiny room with a bed and a chair. He never complained and graced his family with a beautiful gentle spirit as long as I knew him. I see evidence of that gentleness in his grandchildren.

Henry Nathanial Gilbert

It is interesting to note that while Grandmother Wright Nichols was instrumental in the beginning of Garry's and my nine year courtship, it was Grandaddy who "saved the day" at the end of our on-off dating. When we announced our engagement in the Spring of 1966, Dad spent many evenings sulking in the cattle barn reporting to Mom that he was not going to walk his daughter down the aisle of a Catholic Church. When Grandaddy stated that he would be "proud to walk his granddaughter down the aisle," Dad finally acquiesced and did his duty.

These two wonderful human beings, Florence Wright Nichols and Henry Nathaniel Gilbert were powerful influences in my life. Their stark differences were aligned smack dab in the middle through amazing love and sacrifices for their beloved children and grandchildren. Perhaps we "operated" them after all.

School Days

SO MANY MOMS and dads become a bit weepy during late August, as their children step on college campuses, climb on the big yellow bus or hesitate on the steps of junior high or high school for the first time. The same is probably true of most of the kids, themselves, as they tentatively approach the incredible challenges of 21st Century schools.

I think I was born to love school, always have and always will. My schooling unexpectedly started at Hunter School on the Clinton Road near the Indiana border. There was no Kindergarten in Illinois in 1948, when I was 5 years old, and many days, I just hopped onto the bus with my first grade brother, and sat in the one-room school house learning along with the handful of kids in Grades 1-8. But the real deal came the following year, when I stepped into the yellow bus and headed in the opposite direction to the small town of Vermilion, IL and its two story brick building called Vermilion Elementary School. The school was originally built in 1911 as a high school with three teachers in four classrooms, and eventually converted to an 8 room elementary school. Gertrude Harkness was my first grade teacher and I loved her. Her room held treasures everywhere. There was a green metal sandbox with bench seats on each side. Beautifully printed letters framed the top of the blackboard. I had my own desk and carefully placed the first grade books inside that Mom and Dad paid a small rental fee for me to use that year. I think I brought new pencils and crayons for my desk, but kleenex, rulers, chalk and ink wells were furnished by the school. Miss Harkness was not married and dressed very conservatively with a bun on the back of her head, but within her circle of love for children and no nonsense teaching, I learned to read, solve problems and get along with others.

Vermilion Elementary School, Vermilion, Illinois

I remember all of my elementary teachers (Mrs. Shirar, 2nd; Miss Dennis, 3rd; Miss Doty, 4th; Mr. Del Ponte, 5th; Mrs. Tiffin, 6th; Mrs. Jenkins, 7th) and followed the eighth grade teacher, Mr. Gifford to the brand new Crestwood Elementary near Paris, a consolidation of all the rural schools. Miss Dennis was surely my favorite teacher. She was young, energetic and happy all the time. Her learning tasks were fun and we went on many field trips, including a special one to the Maple Syrup Farm. On that trip, Mom drove a carful of my classmates and one of my male classmates held my hand in the back seat. I also tell my grandchildren what happened to me in fifth grade, when I dropped my pencil on the floor and Mr. Del Ponte (a red-haired excitable Italian) made me write on the blackboard 100 times, "I will be less noisy in class!" I had to stand on a stool to reach the top of the blackboard. Things have changed.

I also appreciated Mr. Higgins, the school janitor. He always had a smile and whatever anyone needed, he managed to find or fix. My favorite day of the year was Valentine's Day. Everyone made homemade valentines and a valentine box. We made cards for everyone in the class, so no one felt left out. In fifth grade, Bobby Ross gave me a few chocolate covered cherries on Valentine's Day. I did not care for him or chocolate covered cherries, so I hid them in someone else's desk.

Mom was almost always a room mother for one of her kids. I was very proud when she was my room mother. She was so kind to all of the kids and she made great cookies and cupcakes for my classmates.

Some of my favorite memories swirl around recess, when we were on the swings, the giant slide or we played baseball, dodge ball, or a thousand other group games. I will never forget the day we second graders played baseball, and I wet my pants. I can still visualize the light yellow tiered skirt I was wearing that awful day. Mom had made that skirt and I tied my sweater around my waist so the wet spot wouldn't show. I was mortified! When we could do anything we wanted at recess, I enjoyed the thrill of the merry-go-round, with feet tucked under the iron ring and leaning back to pick up sticks as the merry-go-round whirled. Yikes! Bloody elbows were just a part of the game. There was also a small space under the fire escape on the west side of the building, where I played "house" with my boyfriends.... Tom Tweedy and Sonny Bercaw.

Other favorite times included the annual Halloween parties in the school basement. I can still see first grader Mary Jane Watson running through the basement in her little red devil costume, sobbing at all of the scary creatures. I remember the excitement of dancing in the Christmas Pageant when the primary grades performed the Nutcracker Suite. Mom made my white ballerina tutu trimmed with red sequins for my debut as the Sugar Plum Fairy. My sister was a bright yellow crepe paper flower, performing with many first and second graders in an unforgettable Waltz of the Flowers. Anytime I hear the music of Tchaikovsky's Nutcracker, I can picture the rickety stage propped 12 inches above the basement floor in our school, now long gone. Yet another "fave" activity was walking down the alley to the candy store on Vermilion's main street during noon recess. I always got the flat sticky white taffy because it lasted a long time.

The saddest day of my elementary school days saw the entire student body file silently out of the building and walk slowly across the street to the Vermilion Methodist Church. One of our schoolmates had fallen with a stick in his hand a few days earlier, driving the stick into his eye. He didn't make it. The picture of that little coffin being carried out of the church and the tears of so many remains a poignant memory.

I felt loved, safe and challenged in that old brick school.

The Meeting Will Come to Order

PERHAPS IT IS about having a large space these days to spread out mail, check book, iPad and coffee cups, but the kitchen table seems the perfect place to talk about "big stuff." Decisions about buying a new grill, trading cars, selecting dates for travel to Illinois, Texas, Arizona or California or, perhaps identifying tasks for today's docket are often placed "on the table" before the last breakfast crumbs are swallowed.

Years ago, in the farmhouse kitchen, the table was green and chrome. The morning business between Mom and Dad was frequently interrupted with neighbors arriving to chat or enjoy a cup of coffee. Two memorable kitchen visitors were Arthur, the hired man and neighbor, Wheeler (Doc). My brother, sister and I laughed at hearing "Ar-er" talk. He had a speech articulation impediment and could not enunciate syllables very well, but he always had a great big smile and was most enthusiastic about sharing his perspective on life. He always stood in a corner, ready to go to work when Dad gave the signal. Doc, another frequent kitchen visitor, was a longtime friend and neighbor who lived and farmed down the road and around the corner. I don't even know what their commonalities were, but Doc always had time for a cup of coffee with a little whiskey to jumpstart his day. Dad's whiskey bottle was reserved for Doc and newborn pigs who had been neglected by their mother and needed an extra jolt in their bottles of milk to survive! Perhaps, whisky was essential to Doc's long life as well. There was a lot of laughter, joking and "big talk," as they opined about everything!

THE MEETING WILL COME TO ORDER

The kitchen table also served in a reception capacity, accessible from the back door. All family and visitors were invited to "sit" a spell. The front door was utilized only by salesmen, someone whose car broke down or the Pastor. I don't ever recall the back (or front) door being locked while I was living at the farm but all those who arrived at the farm clearly and loudly announced their arrival with the clanging of bells that hung on the back kitchen door. I would recognize those bells in an instant!

I wonder when Mom and Dad started conducting business at the kitchen table? Mom kept her journals in the cabinet on the side porch at the farm so their proximity to the kitchen table was perfect. Dad never did use a calculator and was extremely proud of his math skills in calculating farm expenses and revenues. Our children still recite Dad's famous saying "a pint's a pound the world around!" How I wish the farm kitchen walls could talk…..imagine the discussions when John U and Florence ran the farm and their only son ran away to get married….and the tragedies that followed with John U's heart attack, their brother-in-law's death in Italy, their young daughter's heartbreaking accidental death and the near loss of the farm to the bank. I wonder how often Mom and Dad's first baby entered the conversation at the kitchen table when no one else was around? Were there ever tears?

Certainly, when my parents' children were gone from the farm and they bought a home in town, business meetings during and after eggs, sausage or bacon and toast sometimes lasted for hours. There were slight variations of the breakfast menu when children and grandchildren were present….biscuits and gravy, sweet petals and homemade doughnuts, but a concern about high cholesterol was destined for the next generation. Coffee was always a part of breakfast and business meetings. Mom poured Dad's coffee most often into a Wedgwood teacup, cream was added and then poured into the saucer to cool off a bit…..and then back into the cup. At the green farm table or the round oak town table, Dad was clearly CEO, but mom was Chief Financial Officer (CFO), Treasurer (paid the bills),

Manager (saw that items were brought up for discussion and execution) and Historian. In the latter role, Mom logged the weather, the crop results, the seed decisions, the cattle purchases and sales, how many chickens, and which of the children or grandchildren checked in on a particular day in her treasured journals. Mom pretty much kept to the facts….rain or snowfall for the day….number of cattle off to market….or number of tomatoes canned the day before. In later years, Mom was also Transport Official, delivering Dad to the bank or to suppliers or service providers. Dad insisted on transacting bank business face to face and in later years, he had the "girls" at the bank enter his deposits and withdrawals in his tiny bank book. They were rewarded with a holiday box of candy. He insisted that bills be paid immediately and in person. He spent $5 in gas for every 5 – 40 cent stamp he saved over the years…..and defended his time-demanding process with, "you got to look em' in the eye!" Friends and neighbors checked in throughout the years to share information, discuss local news (including the town's local SCANDAL SHEET) and share stories of the "good old days." All who came sat at the kitchen table and ate a cookie or three.

    When Mom and Dad moved to town, their home had a special room complete with office desk and file cabinet, but I don't think much business transpired in what doubled as Mom's sewing room, anchored by her black Singer Sewing Machine. She kept toys for grandchildren in that space and there was a couch and TV for grandchildren's shows. The official office remained in the kitchen, where the temperature was just right, the coffee was close and the cookie jar was within reach. Maybe the kitchen worked seamlessly since Mom also doubled as Dad's personal waitress and official greeter for spur of the moment guests.

    Perhaps the most significant lesson and memory of my glimpses into their "office business" was their unspoken understanding of who did what, a genuine team created and maintained throughout 73 years of marriage. It was a partnership of respect, built on trust and awareness of balancing (however lopsided) their expectations for each other in order for the team to succeed. Paper and pencil are replaced today with computer, calculator and online banking. Are today's families successful at "operating seamlessly" with microwave efficiency and "no time to spare" family presence at the kitchen table?

There's a Hole in the Bucket

WHAT DOES IT take to fill a bucket? Farm kids use buckets for plenty of things. Water, corn, eggs, green beans, hedge apples, persimmons, hickory nuts, morel mushrooms, tomatoes, milk, dirt and dog food for sure....but what about the things you can't hold in your hands or see, but yet, somehow fill the buckets of your heart and soul with joy? Growing up, one of my most memorable artistic "bucket fillers" was dance, a joyful activity initiated in a town basement under the Kook and Link Drug Store and culminating on the stage of Paris High School auditorium. I remember when……

Dozens of children (mostly girls....a few young boys), crawled out the tall window of the Biology Room, scampered up the outside fire escape at Paris High School and slipped through an Exit door leading to the Auditorium's backstage. This rather perilous journey ensured that we avoided being seen by the audience since there was no backstairs. As the curtain lifted for the finale of the annual Crabtree Dance Recital, smiling young dancers strutted onto the auditorium stage, singing...."You shall have dancing wherever you go.....!" Under the bright theater lights, at least one hundred 3-16 year-olds sang enthusiastically, at nearly crescendo level following an evening of dancing to a full house and thundering applause. Beautiful bouquets of roses were placed in the arms of the Crabtree sisters—Miss Ethel Marie, dance teacher and Miss Anne, piano accompanist—and the curtain descended over another sparkling performance. Dressed in brightly colored costumes of satin, sequins and scratchy net, my sister and I were part of the annual Recital for nearly a decade in the 50's.

Dance lessons began when I was six years old in Paris, Illinois as the lithe, hair-pulled-back-and-coiled-on-top-of-the-head, posture-perfect Miss Ethel Marie introduced new ways for the feet, arms, hands, head and torso to curve and point. We were gifted with the discipline of dance as we practiced the positions and steps of ballet, the rhythm of tap, and the graceful elegance and pain of dancing on our toes. Heading to our weekly lessons, we clattered down the steps into the basement below a thriving drug store (at the corner of Central and Wood Streets) to enter Miss Ethel Marie's Dance Studio. We carried small cardboard suitcases holding ballet and tap shoes and eventually, the coveted pink satin toe shoes. We wore white, sleeveless sailcloth frocks (sewn by our mothers) trimmed at square necklines with red rickrack, until we graduated to black leotards… another coveted milestone. Every May, we stepped onto a real stage to display our progress in mastering the arabesque and "shuffle, ball change" to perform the annual dance recital in the high school auditorium (no out-of-town travel competitions in those days).

In the same high school with the multi-use fire escape, I was a 14 year old freshman settled in one of the back rows of the auditorium (seniors got the front rows even though they were bigger and blocked our view of the stage). All 800 students were gathered for a monthly Lyceum Program. The program featured four men singing a variety of songs with the encore a lively rendition of *Rocka' My Soul In The Bosom of Abraham*. The singing group challenged the high school audience to mimic the same lyric four times, with each rendition having a different rhythm. If……we were successful all four times, the foursome promised to buy lunch for the entire student body! The young men sang the lyric first and 800 high school students repeated it. Each time there was a different rhythm, and the students matched the cadence perfectly. On the fourth and final variation, students were on the edge of their seats! I remember the look, the feel and the excitement present in the auditorium that day. Everyone was engaged….

everyone was tasting "the free lunch!" I will never forget the "unity" among my classmates. Well... several of my fellow students missed the extended "rest" after "Rocka my......" and lunch was "off the table." We didn't succeed, but an amazing "unity" spread throughout the auditorium that day as we experienced "oneness," ...a feeling of connection putting forth unified best effort toward a common goal. I was lifted that morning in a "hot air balloon" kind of way! Not one student's "WE ARE ONE" bucket was empty that day!

My siblings and I were blessed with parents, extended family and farm neighbors who intuitively understood that babies start performing practically at birth when they figure out what it takes to make adults smile and laugh. In those days, I don't think parents were intentional about teaching us the value of positive interactions, but classrooms across the country later adopted the strategy of "filling character buckets" with kind thoughts and deeds. Building character "back in the day" occurred rather spontaneously as we performed, raced, jumped, pirouetted, sang, conversed and were supported in well-guided efforts to become courageous, confident and respectful. Filling our buckets occurred while we were connecting with classmates, and friends and their families, strengthening our sense of belonging and learning how to face vulnerability. The pleasant and continuous "plops" in the character bucket far outweighed the negative "misses," and the buckets of self-esteem continued to fill. Our caregivers at home, school, church and in the community were present, engaged and paying attention. Their huge smiles, encouragement and enthusiastic applause throughout those early years, laid the groundwork for more challenging "life dances" that lay ahead.

Sometimes our parents' buckets held drops of tears...most of which reflected pride in their children's accomplishments. Sometimes our own buckets held tears of disappointment or frustration. But, Mom and Dad seemed to understand that when children are encouraged and supported as they learn to sing or dance or play ball, especially under the lights of a gymnasium or auditorium, and adults are in attendance as enthusiastic spectators, everyone's bucket fills. The question of buckets that never seem to fill, no matter what gets added, remains a mystery. Even after more than 78 years of adding to my own personal bucket, there still seems to be room for more! Perhaps, dear Liza, there's a "hole!"

Reap What You Sow

NOTHING SAYS FALL to me like the sight of a combine steadily crawling along the dried, droopy corn rows, separating the ears of corn from their stalks and spilling shelled corn into hoppers, trucks or wagons. In nearby fields, dried bean plants, patiently wait for the appropriate moisture content, portraying an ending....to this year's crops, a beginning....of dollars for the coming year and a point in time to "reap what you have sown." It would be so different, living in a part of the country where the harvest focuses on fruits and vegetables during different seasons of the year. Thank goodness, Minnesota and Illinois share a midwest harvesting of corn and beans. Harvest, to me, is October, fall colors. shorter days, brisk cool air and the sounds and lights of farm equipment running late into each night when the weather is right.

My early harvest "helper" position was usually near the cattle barn, watching Mom or Dad pull the tail gate levers at the back of the big red wagon. Ears of corn cascaded onto the Hiker's moving chains up and into the opening on the barn roof, filling up the corn cribs to feed our cattle all winter. I loved riding with Dad on the tractor, with the Corn Picker trailing behind, but I did not like riding in or near the bean/grain hopper. As the hopper filled, I was always covered with chaff and oat bugs that crawled all over my arms and legs as the dust flew everywhere and made every part of my body itch. I remember many nights when the tractor headlights moved along the field rows for hours into the dark night, trying to outmaneuver rain or hail. I can still sense the somber, "lost" feeling after a hail storm, although I did not, at that time, understand the financial significance of the "permanently damaged crops." Mom and Dad carried that burden without making their children absorb the worry accompanying a steep decline in annual revenue. Budgeting without a regular revenue stream, resulted in a complex partnership with the local banks. What trust there must have been, and still must exist between bankers and farmers! I think I understand the underlying success of Dad's financial negotiations, "ya' got to look 'em in the eye!"

What a difference 60 years can make! The air surrounding the driver of the modern Combine Harvester is cooled, dust and bug-free, and filled with music, news or phone conversation with those harvesting crops all over one's farmland. Today's Combine drivers collect 12 rows or more of corn, beans or other grains in one sweep while their young children may be napping in the back corners of the cool, quiet cab.

Today, enormous wagons or trucks travel alongside the Combines, loading up corn that has already been shelled on its way into the wagon or truck-bed. Semi-trucks wait at the end of the field to haul the grains to storage bins, grain elevators or other holding tanks. In Dad's early years, grains were hauled to the Elevators by tractor and wagon or truck. I will always associate Grain Elevators with Harold Adams, manager of the County Elevator. The easy camaraderie between Dad and Harold always made me feel happy. All I remember in the stark, colorless Elevator Office is Harold's unique laugh and delight in teasing his friend, U.G., in front of his kids as Harold shared "the joke of the day" and quoted the "price of the day."

The sleek green or red Combine Harvesters of today, worth hundreds of thousands of dollars, have advanced exponentially in size, structure, function and electronic complexity. A lot of the guesswork in farming has been resolved with advanced computer technology that has my head spinning. Modern Combine Harvesters perform four separate harvesting functions—reaping, threshing, gathering and winnowing into a single process ...quite a mechanical leap since the days of our manual corn sheller, hand cranking, shelling one ear at a time. The bucket under the sheller was slowly filled with corn and carried to the chickens or turkeys to feed hungry fowl. A bucketful of corn was occasionally set aside in late October for Halloween "tricks!" The ancient sheller occupies a special place in my memory and on our side porch reminding me of my farm girl days.

Harvest is "make or break" time for farmers, and there continues to be truckloads of relief upon reaching the end of the planting, growing and harvesting seasons. Even during droughts or excessive rain, it is hard to turn one's back on the fulfilling occupation of farming. When Mom and Dad "achieved" the Farm Bureau "200 bushels of corn per acre award," it was surely equivalent to a Pulitzer Best Book, Television Emmy or Nobel Peace prize. Our parents worked unquestionably hard in their chosen livelihood of farming to "sow productive seeds," maximizing every opportunity to "reap" the most profitable harvest. Interestingly enough, without even being overtly conscious of their parenting efforts, they planted and cultivated values, beliefs and principles of a loving, ethical, strong family. In harvest over a lifetime, Mom and Dad proudly "reaped what they had so diligently, yet naturally sown."

And let us not become weary of doing good, for at the proper time we will reap a harvest if we do not give up. Galatians 6:9

WIPE AWAY EVERY TEAR

Trust on the Caring Bridge

WE MISS HER. We didn't always understand her, but we loved her and take solace in the knowledge that God took her to live with Him because we know without a doubt, she believed in Him. My husband's only sibling, Nancy, left us October 16, 2007. Garry took her hand that final morning, and with our youngest daughter at his side, spoke her name. She quietly slipped away with the awareness that family stood beside her. Her ten years of fighting Mantle Cell Lymphoma were over, but the journey was laced with gratitude toward the medical professionals who gifted her with a healthy, optimistic quality of life throughout her scary, anxious journey.

I am painfully aware of how quickly time has flown as I reread the poignant reflections on her Caring Bridge site in the final days before her death.

October 12th...*Nancy spent the day visiting with her nephew and his family. John (age 4) loved the balloons sent by his aunt, residing in England. Nancy shared with Father Bennett (the wonderful Irish priest from Dublin...whom Nancy's niece described as "Jesus walking into the room")...that she was prepared. Nancy's brother was rendered speechless, heart bursting, as Father Bennett sang an Irish hymn to his sister.*

October 13th....*Nancy asks to move her treatment plan to Comfort Care. She anxiously awaits seeing her niece, who will arrive from England the next day.*

October 15th...*Today was a milestone in many ways for Nancy.*

FATHER, MAY I...

Her grandniece, was able to spend her eighth birthday visiting "Nanny." The nursing staff all signed a birthday card, brought her a cupcake and we all sang happy birthday. Skipping school that day brought very special privileges.

Dr. Witzig had been Nancy's hero for these past 10 years, and late into the night, prior to her death, he sat beside her bed for a long time sharing his admiration of her courage and determination as they fought together for a solution to this terminal cancer. Nancy learned that she would be making news on the international scene in the future. Her mantle cells would be cultured and grown in Dr. Witzig's research lab for future study. The cells develop a line of their own identity and would be identified as "NH1." We will be forever grateful for witnessing an incredible portrayal of the Hippocratic Oath ("in purity and according to divine law will I carry out my life and my art") as Dr. Witzig sat by her bedside preparing Nancy for peace. Her calm spirit...and his... soothed our aching hearts.

On October 22nd, in her home town of Terre Haute, Indiana, at Sacred Heart Church, we described a unique life, well-lived, in the following eulogy for Nancy in the presence of family and friends who gathered to celebrate her life.

When Paul wrote to the Philippians he said, "always be full of joy in the Lord...I say it again, rejoice! Let everyone see that you are unselfish and considerate in all you do." To say that our Nancy was considerate would be an understatement. Her generosity is legendary. She was "Aunt Nancy" first and foremost, not only to her nephew, nieces, and seven great nieces and nephews, but she was "Aunt Nancy" to the many children of her friends and co-workers. She showered all of them with her attention, special gifts and most of all, her love.

That same unselfish consideration was bestowed upon her old friends from the early Terre Haute years...her work friends from Eli Lilly...new friends in St. Cloud...and the hundreds of friends she made throughout her 61 years of zestful, vivacious, spirited and spunky living. She was the perfect travel companion...just ask her nieces and nephew and many friends. She's been described as funky...a real "hoot" and how she loved the unusual! Nancy shopped at places like "Beached Whale," " Cravings," and even worked at a clothing store called "Pink Lime." She was a great cook and the ultimate hostess. One of our favorite responses on the Caring Bridge site occurred when Nancy was struggling for life in Mayo's Intensive Care Unit. Her brother spent his birthday at her bedside, and Nancy, who has been described on the web site as wonder woman, trooper, fashion queen, tough cookie and "miss modern," managed to arrange a birthday party, shopped for a cupcake from the hospital cafeteria and organized a birthday choir of nurses. Later, on the Caring Bridge, friend Gus's wife Susie incredulously noted that Nancy is probably the only person ever to have "shopped" from ICU.

Nancy joyfully experienced life in "living color." Her laugh and beautiful smile built friendships around the world at tennis camp, the Disney Wine Bar, restaurants in Arizona, the Indy 500 race track and the stands at Indiana Pacer and Colt games. Her friendship extended to those who cleaned her rooms in the Rochester hotels to those who poked her with thousands of needles to those who faced hard and challenging times in their personal lives. One of those friends was a teen-age boy named Luke, a special St. Cloud family friend, who lost his leg and eventually his life to cancer. One of Nancy's memorials honored Luke, one of the inspiring lives from which the Quiet Oaks Hospice House in St. Cloud took root.

In Paul's letter, he also advises the Philippians not to worry about anything; instead, "pray about everything; tell God your needs." All of the prayers for peace, love, healing, strength, courage and faithfulness were answered. Nancy placed her trust in God...her caregivers...her doctors...her family and her friends and she was at peace.

Finally in his letter, Paul reminds the Philippians..."and don't forget to thank Him for his answers." We thank God for our time with Nancy. We thank God for showing her how to be the "World's Best Aunt" to so many children. As her friend Dick noted on Caring Bridge, Nancy "committed to living life to the fullest by sharing her joy with all that surrounded her." And so we thank God, for sharing that joy *with all of us. Thank you, God, for teaching us life lessons through Nancy: Don't complain, live life to its fullest, always be kind, celebrate your own style and fill your days with the joys of family and wonderful friends. "Let everyone see that you are unselfish and considerate in all you do," said Paul. And thank you, God, for the healing of relationships that will continue to be part of Nancy's legacy. It takes courage to heal broken spirits, to seek forgiveness, to reach out to others in need, to think about things that are pure and lovely and to dwell on the fine, good things in others. Nancy's legacy is one of courage.*

Her brother and I and our children are grateful for the opportunity to walk with Nancy as she completed her journey to the gates of Heaven. Our family, including her beloved cousins, pray that Nancy will be an eternal reminder of the quest for joy... to pray about everything...and to be thankful for God's answers to our prayers. If we can do those things, God's peace will surely surround us.

Angels Among Us

MY EARLY MEMORIES of "religion" bring to mind the kind pastors of the First United Methodist Church in the 50's and 60's, whose presence in the pulpit was calm and respectful. Reverend Lewis D. Hopper and his diminutive wife, Maude, are remembered as positive and supportive. They lingered at the conclusion of church near the sanctuary exit to "connect," mingling at potlucks in the church basement or listening intently in the privacy of the Pastor's office. Both Reverend Hopper and Maude connected spiritually in one way or another with what seemed like a thousand men, women and children focused attentively each Sunday in the dark mahogany pews of the Methodist Church in Paris, IL.

Reverend Clarence Nordling was Pastor when I was in sixth grade. He presented a Confirmation Bible, with my name embossed in gold on the white cover. Perhaps the most significant pastoral religious intervention in my life occurred when Assistant Methodist Pastor Herb Thompson stood with Catholic Priest, Father James McBarron in 1966 and united my husband and I in marriage at Sacred Heart Church in Terre Haute, Indiana. It was a short, emotionally-charged event (because of "mixed marriage"protocol), but we stepped out of that church, initiating a marriage lasting 55 years to date....and we're still counting! It is my understanding that young Methodist Pastor Thompson initiated a conversation with my "doubting Thomas" Dad and persuaded him to accept his role as father of the bride and walk me down the aisle of a Roman Catholic Church.

FATHER, MAY I...

Our faith, as a couple today has been guided by our life experiences, some within the First United Methodist Church in Paris and even more through nearly 50 years of adult and active membership in St. Paul's Catholic Church in St. Cloud, MN. Woven throughout those years are relationships, learning opportunities and experiences that have shaped and deepened our faith. We continue to have questions and seek answers as our life together unfolds. We are guided by conversations with family members and friends, <u>Bible</u> studies, educational opportunities and visits to spiritual places.....the Chapel perched on a cliff in Sedona, AZ, the St. John's Bible exhibit, and a recent visit to Canyon DeShelly, where God's plan is further revealed through Navajo history. Of no small consequence, is the ever growing wisdom of our children and grandchildren as it profoundly enlightens our spiritual journey.

I replaced my Confirmation Bible with a paperback version, titled <u>The Word of God Alive & Active</u> (today's English Version from the American Bible Society). When we visit Arizona, I enjoy listening to the different phraseology from the bibles of my Lutheran bible study friends. I also appreciate my Bible's easy references to scripture that give direction to personal struggles, needs, and celebrations.

In the early 90's, a gift certificate for a "week-end away" was presented to my husband and I by our college-age children. They practically had to arm-wrestle us to attend TEC 243 (Together Encountering Christ), a week-end retreat at a church "classroom" site in Belle Prairie, MN. They refused to answer our questions about what the week-end involved, saying "we can't tell you!" My husband and I were pretty sure we were headed for some kind of cult experience..."what were all the secrets about?" We were not excited about spending a week-end sleeping on bunk beds in a crowded room and were even less so when we arrived and discovered the signs that advised us to conserve water, placed strategically over the toilets...."if it's yellow, let it mellow; if it's brown, flush it down!"

The first day was "Die Day," a day centered on the death of Jesus Christ. We reflected on many aspects of our lives, focusing on better relationships with God, self, and others. My husband and I were facing the "empty nest," and wondered what that might mean for life going forward, as well as our relationship with each other. The experience blossomed with each passing hour.

On Day Two (Rise Day), we celebrated the presence of God's love in our lives with a huge surprise! At one point, all of the TEC volunteers (who cooked, cleaned and took care of us) filed into the meeting room, singing Kenny Rogers' hit song, "Angels Among Us." And to our total amazement, there stood two of our college age children! With huge "Gotcha Grins," they joined us for a few brief moments, truly enjoying the surprise and teasing us with, "You ain't seen nothin' yet!" And they were right. That evening, we were led (with eyes closed) in circles within a darkened gymnasium and into a celebration where, honestly, I thought my heart would burst. I can only say, there was a light and a love "in that room" that could only have been God, Himself, among us.

Our final day was "Go Day," a day aimed at exploring God's continuous call to spread the Good News of Jesus. A couple of years later, I had the opportunity to share TEC 245 with Brian Klinefelter, his future wife, Wendy and future mother-in-law, Zoe Schneider. It was customary to write in one another's Bibles during the TEC weekend, and I treasure all the voices, who encouraged me to find joy in <u>all things</u>. Zoe wrote ... "I'm so glad we had this chance to serve the Lord and our children together!" Wendy wrote, "We have some really happy times to look forward to...I can't wait!"

The week-end was filled with unforgettable, beautiful friendship, heart-wrenching stories, lessons of humility, joyful music, prayerful guidance and honest reflection. And our children were right, the culmination of the week-end delivered an emotional high that brought indescribable joyful gratitude for Jesus' love. I cannot spoil the surprise for others by describing it here. The feeling of being one with God stays with us today.

But.... just when I thought I had reached some kind of pinnacle through this humbling religious experience delivered in a sparse set of rooms with so many strangers....there was more to the story. A couple of years later, I returned to the TEC center. TEC 245 brought the amazing joy of serving as our youngest daughter's angel as part of the volunteer Wheat Team. I will never, ever forget my daughter's affirming, loving words in that extraordinary week-end of grace and bonding, *"will you be my best friend forever?"*

God saw a different plan for Brian and Zoe, with whom we shared our love of God and special friendship that week-end. Their untimely deaths still ache.

In January, 2014, Garry and I sat with my brother and sister-in-law in White's Chapel United Methodist Church in Texas, taking in the breath-taking, sparkling Christmas trees, the 200 member choir and two large TV screens displaying hymns, videos, messages and graphic illustrations of the sermon and announcements.The church was inspirational and the cushioned, tiered seating in this beautiful Methodist Church offered comfort and peaceful ambience welcoming its 7,000 members and visitors. The energetic pastors and beautiful music opened our hearts to the Word.

Joy seemed to flow in that church and I was anxious to consider why??? In listing previous joyful moments and events in my life, I think of Christmas mornings, perfect scores on tests, Garry's marriage proposal, pulling into Mom and Dad's driveway at Christmas after the 700 mile drive from St. Cloud, and cradling our three children and each new grandchild in my arms for the very first time... joy seems both big and small and appears to have very little to do with achievement or material possessions.

Special places, encounters and events trigger spiritual renewal, helping me to capture joy. God sends messages reminding us that joy is relative to knowing Him. In the Bible, James noted, "Count it all joy, my brothers, when you meet trials of various kinds," in spite of the fact that it is hard to be joyful when the going gets tough.

Psalm 30:11 reminds us that God always "turns our mourning into dancing. He has loosed my sackcloth and clothed me with gladness." I know that "a joyful heart is good medicine...and a crushed spirit dries up the bones." On those occasions when my spiritual light grows dim, I am learning to pause for prayer placing my trust in God. During TEC 243, Garry wrote in my Bible about the weekend's "power to strengthen our love for one another and our love for family." What a gift! Joy came with a big bang that week-end more than 20 years ago, and again in Texas. But the reality of God's love offers joy around every corner and angels are continually in our midst. My prayer seeks the rekindling of inner light within those we know and love, as well as those who simply share our space on earth. Joy is ours for the taking...and, of course, it was available all along... in our giving.

There is evidence that many answers to life's questions about purpose in this earthly life are discovered within. Our challenge is to remain in pursuit of knowing God. Keep the wisdom coming, dear Jesus! We will always need Your guidance to sow the right seeds in our souls' "rocky ground." Our prayer...both mine and my husband's ...is to keep our minds, hearts and actions engaged as "angels," lighting flames of kindness and hope among God's people.

Albert Schweitzer offers this view ... *"Sometimes our light goes out but is blown again into flame by an encounter with another human being. Each of us owes the deepest thanks to those who have rekindled this inner light."*

The Greatest Things You'll Ever Know

IN DARKEST MOMENTS of grief, desperate for equilibrium, human beings struggle to grasp the meaning of loss and to "see" why something so precious has been taken away. Friends and family may turn to God for help, before or after well-meaning support from others… short on patience for answers. Even when God is approached with a less than grateful heart, He promises to embrace those who seek His comfort. Whatever spiritual beliefs one professes, "invisible" Faith is difficult. Seeking God's answers may involve bartering… "show me"… "a prove it" imperative….an illusive answer to "why?" In the depths of sorrow, humans ache to touch something real, something substantial with clear evidence that a life… a relationship… an effort… meant something.

Finding ourselves in the midst of a psychological hurricane, avalanche, earthquake or mind spiraling out of control, creates a mess with our physical, mental and emotional well-being. In a moment of serious loss, and usually long after, it is natural to ache for something tangible upon which to hang our distress. If only it were possible to grasp something permanent ….anything to steady a broken soul crying out for help. If faith in the guidance of an invisible Deity feels beyond reach, so too does the invisibility of "grace," as tangible comfort is sought. Humanity struggles to be comforted by "that which we cannot see."

Grief typically feels beyond our control...no relief in sight. How many ways can one experience a broken heart? In nearly eight decades of living, some of my most challenging reaches for Faith were tangled in tragic losses of children and young adults. Created so perfectly in His image, I couldn't understand God's snatching these young lives, so filled with promise...so unfair.... too soon. My own sorrow couldn't begin to match the grief consuming their parents and families, as they clung to yesterday's memories, drowned in the reality of the moment and dreading facing a future without their loved ones.

Witnessing the agony of friends who lost their children too soon and deeply saddened, I began to search for a meaningful path to faithfulness. As though it were yesterday, the stories of Paul, Jacob, Luke, Brian, Haley Rose, Jessie and Poppy became stepping stones toward enlightenment of Faith's mystery. These young angels were surely sent by God to bring light to those who were lucky to be nearby.

PAUL

Deep, painful loss ripped my heart on October 7, 1985. I was 42 years old, mother of three young children. My thirteen year old daughter and I stood in front of a shiny, wooden casket gazing at 17 year old high school senior, Paul, who had passed away from Duchenne's disease, a form of muscular dystrophy marked by progressive muscle deterioration. I burst into tears and truly thought my heart was going to shatter. I barely knew Paul, brother to my daughter's classmate, but our local newspaper had endeared this amazing young man to our whole community. The news stories explained that each night during Paul's last weeks, he held a "family meeting" at home to which family members and friends were invited to share their feelings and thoughts. Paul assured all who came that "God is with me."

Paul's pastor shared these thoughts. "Paul is not afraid to die. He knows the truth —that he will enter into a new life without handicap and without concern about the future. Suffering is a mystery and people like Paul help us find meaning in suffering. Acceptance of pain can lead to glory. Paul is ready to come home when the Lord calls him."

Paul expressed his gratitude for many people, appreciating whatever time he had left, yet "baffled why people with good health didn't make the most of their lives." Paul's legacy for so many was one of **courage.** Facing loss, challenge or brokenness ultimately requires a strong spirit and an invisible faith. Jesus reminds us in Psalms 27...

The Lord protects me from all danger; I will never be afraid.

JACOB

During a teacher inservice on October 23, 1989, middle school principal, Ray, announced that one of our students at North Middle School had been abducted the previous night. Throughout the upper midwest and eventually across the country, the story of Jacob Wetterling, an 11 year old who was kidnapped while on an errand with two friends to pick up a movie, captured the attention of parents, school personnel and law enforcement. In the days and weeks that followed, nearly everyone in central Minnesota was involved in the search, scouring every inch of the area, distributing folders, supporting Jacob's family and one another as we waited.....and waited....and waited. So many tears were shed as we all coped with loss of childhood, as we had known it, in our community. An image, frozen in time, remains in my mind, of the hundreds of community members lining both sides of Highway 77, connecting the 8 mile stretch between St. Cloud and St. Joseph, Jacob's hometown. We held hands, shed tears and sang Red Grammer's "Listen, To Your Heart" as the song and hundreds of silent prayers were sent skyward. Jacob's parents formed the Jacob Wetterling Foundation, which became the Jacob Wetterling Resource Center "to educate the public about who takes children, how they do it and what each of us can do to stop it." The Bridge of Hope, a crossing of the Mississippi River near St. Cloud was named in Jacob's honor. It took 27 long years to solve the mystery of Jacob's disappearance, when the abductor, a local resident, finally confessed. Jacob was shot and lost his life the night he was abducted. His remains were recovered September 1, 2016.

Jacob's legacy of hope for the safety of all children.....continues to remain strong. So many in the community cared, took action in the midst of fear, and continue to keep their protective arms around Jacob's family and all children. Jacob's Hope lives on, as new laws are implemented and community actions are put in place to insure the safety of children. In Psalm 33:22, the faithful ask...

May your unfailing love be with us, Lord, even as we put our hope in you.

BRIAN

On January 29, 1996, as our family watched the late evening news, an anchor reported the shooting of a St. Joseph police officer. TV cameras filled our screen with blinking red and blue lights. Minutes earlier, seventeen year old Tiffany was driving through St. Joseph on her way to a friend's home after work. She saw a police car's flashing lights, crept along the icy highway and witnessed an officer fall to the pavement at the side of a white truck. With amazing presence of mind, this young driver U-turned in the median and blocked oncoming traffic with her car. Tiffany knelt beside Officer Brian Klinefelter, comforting him while waiting for help to arrive. Officers, alerted to the traffic stop, responded immediately and quickly arrived at the scene. In minutes, a nurse arrived to minister to the bleeding, unconscious officer.

Confirmation of the victim as Officer Klinefelter, brother of our daughter's fiancé, came quickly and our family bolted to the St. Cloud hospital. The long wait for Brian's dad to arrive from Fargo was excruciating. Brian succumbed to the gunshot wounds. Tightly grasped hands, in a circle of family love surrounding Brian, conveyed peace and God's presence during Pastor Jerry's heartfelt prayer. Heartbreaking, tearful good-byes and memories of the ensuing days are forever captured in my heart. More than 5,000 officers arrived at the College of St. Benedict for Brian's service, along with hundreds of family and community members walking silently to the CSB Center, tears frozen and shivering on the frigid 29 below zero February day. The mournful bagpipes honored a peacekeeper who had protected us all. The powerful, faith-filled words of his father celebrated Brian's 26 years of "do unto others....." living and providing extraordinary, out-of-the box service, protecting and enhancing life in his small community. Jesus gave His life so that our sins may be forgiven. Brian... beloved son, brother, husband and brand-new father, sacrificed his life for a better world, as well.

Faith sustained the Klinefelter family, and twenty-three years later, as Brian's dad, Dave, faced death from cancer and lay in the St. Cloud Hospital, an angel joined the family at Dave's bedside. Knowing that death was very near, clothed in white, RN Brenda, lovingly and knowingly arranged Dave's transfer to the beautiful, rural hospice care home, Quiet Oaks. Brenda knew that the gift of saying good-bye in a comfortable, peaceful environment with the whole family gathered, needed to happen. This atypical patient transfer was not "procedure" for patients who were expected to live less than 48 hours. The angel in white intervened and made it happen.

In 1996, Brian was denied the opportunity to say good-bye to those he loved. The same angel, who knelt on the freezing pavement at Brian's side 23 years earlier, as he fought for his life, stood by Brian's father's bedside, determined to orchestrate a loving "farewell to family." Nurse Brenda arranged for Dave's move to Quiet Oaks Hospice House for a quiet, peaceful good-bye, allowing the family to gently "tie the ribbons," reuniting father and son. Our faith in God looks beyond our senses, and sees, that God is in the midst of our circumstances working His will.

God wants us to see Him as He sees Himself—"as a Lamp shining in a dark place." (2 Peter 1:19)

LUKE

What an inspiration this happy, loving, kind, smart, handsome, brave young man was. This amazing 23 year old was a devoted son, grandson, brother, nephew, friend and husband who never stopped showing others how to live until God called him home on June 14, 2004. Luke endured long, painful hours of physical therapy, the loss of a leg and years of cancer pain and hospital stays. But he spent many more hours enjoying his family, completing a college career, marrying the love of his life, fulfilling a visit with his "Grant A Wish" idol, Robin Williams, traveling with his brother, and loving his parents, brother, wife and friends.

Luke's amazing humor continues to inspire me as I recall a favorite interaction. During a shared Thanksgiving Dinner with Luke's family, he was interested in learning about our family's traditions and formalities. I shared one example of proper etiquette during a "fancy" dinner that involved always passing the salt and pepper together at the table, even if only one was requested. Later, when Luke helped clear the table, he was beaming as he brought the salt and pepper shakers into the kitchen, saying… "Look… they are still married!!"

Luke accepted his approaching death with such grace, asking his family and friends to remember him whenever we heard the well-known Louis Armstrong song, "What A Wonderful World." Luke's music teacher, Ruth LaDuke sang a beautiful rendition at Luke's memorial service. Oh my, what so many learned from Luke's "joy" in living! I could "see" Luke's faith wherever he walked or connected with others. In Psalm 16:11, God shares this joy through His followers, and most assuredly, Luke understood…

You make known to me the path of life; in your presence there is fullness of joy; at your right hand are pleasures forevermore.

HAYLEY ROSE

Hayley Rose, a beautiful newborn, denied that first breath on October 17, 2007, was tenderly held for precious moments in the arms of loving, devastated parents and grandparents. Days, months and years of struggle to find peace, followed Hayley Rose's death. In one tiny effort to mend broken hearts, the family identified the dragonfly as symbolic of Haley Rose's heavenly wings. Watching tiny wings, as dragonflies flew in and out of family space, brought smiles and tears of remembrance to those who loved her. Yet, God had more to His plan.

The day before Haley Rose's birth and death, my sister-in-law, Nancy, relinquished her 61 years of life to God. On October 16, 2007 in the Mayo Hospital, Nancy's ten year roller coaster battle with Mantle Cell Lymphoma came to an end. Her brother, Garry, held her hand during her final breaths, grateful for family memories and closing the door on a long, loving commitment to his sister's well-being. He choked out a tearful farewell to his only sibling, releasing her to a life without struggle. Little did we know that God needed Nancy the next day to carry a tiny baby girl to heaven.

Nancy never married….God must have known how much she loved children. We know what an amazing job she did "spicing up" life for our children. In His infinite wisdom God gently placed a tiny baby into Nancy's loving arms until Camille and Dean could hold Haley Rose once again.

How lucky I am to be [someone] that makes saying goodbye so hard.

(A.A. Milne, <u>Winnie The Pooh</u>)

JESSICA

On July 10, 2021, God called home another young adult, who had faced life throughout her 44 years with courage, determination, optimism and humor. There were trials, heartaches, and challenges along with love, joy and successes. Jessica met the highs and lows, the traps and opportunities with ferocity and gentleness. She was loved and "cheered on" by many.

It had been many years since I had seen Jessica, but from the day her mother introduced us, I can hear Jessica's voice advising, "don't silence the beat in your heart…drum so everyone hears you!" Beautiful, vibrant Jessie sought better lives for homeless, mentally challenged and aging human beings. Jessica was brilliant, enjoyed those whose lives intersected with hers and undeniably adored her young daughter. Jessie loved animals and God had a special mission for her, too......

The answer to "why?" will be a long time coming, even though Jessica unselfishly fulfilled God's advice written in Galatians 6:2.

Carry each other's burdens and so you will fulfill the law of Christ.

POPPY

Two days after Jessica courageously succumbed to "no more," our sweet little tricolor King Charles Cavalier grand-dog, 8 Poppy, lost her short battle with Myasthenia Gravis. Both Haley Rose and Poppy have shown us there is no time frame for developing an intensity of feeling with those we love. After four short years of "best puppy friend ever," the onslaught of this aggressive neuromuscular disorder left no hope for recovery. We loved Poppy the moment she landed in our laps and relished her snuggles, kisses, walks, playtime, overnights and sharing Tillamook Ice Cream. The joy expressed in her swishing tail and quiet enjoyment of gentle caresses are securely tucked into our memory box. As Poppy entered the Kingdom of Heaven, assuredly in Jessica's arms, the smile on Jessie's face and the wag in Poppy's tail surely illuminated the heavenly gates as God welcomed this well-loved twosome.

Poppy came into our lives, left paw prints on our hearts and we are forever changed.

Paul, Jacob, Brian, Luke, Haley Rose, Jessie and Poppy have gifted many with the opportunity for insight into the "invisible." My faith grows as God reveals ways to support others experiencing acute, all-encompassing pain. I believe that God expects us to understand that not only does grief reflect who and what we love, it can be further intensified by guilt (I could have done more! I didn't do the right things!) Or, if a relationship is difficult or circumstances are out of one's control, confusion is bound to follow. Faith's journey requires opening and executing the "care package," individually and lovingly assembled by our Savior.

FATHER, MAY I...

My faith in the "unseen" grows through all that is inspired by these young champions, including the promise that God walks beside us in our "brokenness." He signals that message through Paul's strength, Haley Rose's promise, Jacob's hope, Brian's kindness, Jessie's courage and Poppy's genuine joy. I cherish each one of them. I smile because I knew them.

In the Netflix film, Klaus," A selfish postman and a reclusive toymaker form an unlikely friendship, delivering joy to a cold, dark town that desperately needs it. In the film's theme song, "Invisible," vocalist Zara Larsson gives credence to invisibility of Faith...

You can't take it, steal it

But you can always feel it

The greatest things you'll ever know

Are invisible........

"Help me, God, to embrace the invisibility of Faith." I believe that it is one of the greatest things I will ever know.

We Are The Champions

Ordinary Olympians

JUST WHAT DOES it mean to be an Olympian? It's a question worth pondering whenever the Olympic Games dominate television programming. The athletes' faces reflect intense emotion as they step onto the podium to accept medals in exchange for years of pain, struggle and perseverance. Every competitor is "golden," after sometimes decades of intense dedication and sacrifice aimed at "being the best," and more than likely, "next best" by hundredths of seconds.

As a young girl, I dreamed of being an Olympic Ice Skater. Imagine how thrilled I was when Mom told me that we were related to 1976 Olympic Gold Medalist Dorothy Hamill! Could it be true that mom's grandfather, James Barr and Dorothy's paternal grandfather were brothers? Mom remembered when Dorothy's father, Chalmers Hamill, visited our home town many years ago as a young boy.

Since it was impossible for the pond on the farm to freeze smooth enough to allow for triple axels and double-toe loops,.... I decided to consider swimming. Perhaps it started in the hog waller behind the cattle barn where a "larger than life" mud puddle accommodated hogs "wallering" in gooey mud and #&@*! My siblings and I cooled ourselves, in that same "pool," on hot summer days. Rare summer trips to the Happyland swimming pool in a nearby Indiana town and brief swim lessons at Twin Lakes Park in Paris didn't get me any closer to the podium. I really wanted to be a beautiful swimmer like my mother and even resorted to "cheating" during swim ability testing at 4-H camp. We were required to take swimming tests to determine our

FATHER, MAY I...

swim levels as a "blue, red or white" swimmer. I pretended to swim the full 100 yards so that I would be classified as a "blue" swimmer. After three or four strokes I planted my feet in the sand and boosted myself forward. I guess I didn't fool the counselors....I didn't even qualify at the lowest level.

I made one last attempt to learn to swim during a one-credit course in the Indiana State University pool, where I had to be "hooked" by the instructor when a cramp paralyzed my leg as a college sophomore. So much for my Olympic quest. I am so proud of all of our grandchildren, who have endured the rigor of many swim lessons. All nine of them could pass the 100 yard standard leaving Mimi stuck in the sand!

When our children were in the lower elementary grades, I decided to host a Backyard Olympics at our St. Cloud home. We invited all the neighborhood kids and set up many events for pint-sized Olympians. Ages ranged from 18 months to 9 years. Events included (1) "walking the platform" set up on top of two small step ladders without falling off; (2) jumping rope; (3) speed walking around the block; (4) hula hoop endurance; and (5) hopping, skipping and walking backwards. During the award ceremony, participants waved tiny American flags and sang the Star Spangled Banner. Red, white and blue ribbons with attached medals (Gerber Baby Food Lids sprayed with gold paint) were proudly placed around their necks as they stood on wooden boards supported by red bricks. I think it was the best event I ever planned!

In my mind, real Olympians practice, sweat, and aim for high levels of performance every day in the homes of families throughout our nation. Parents and often grandparents strive every day for tiny victories in the challenging work of raising children. There is little cheering....there are no medals....and giving up is not an option. It is hard to keep one's eyes on the goal through years of trial and error, financial challenge, unforeseen bends in the road and sheer exhaustion. Olympic Champions endure uncountable falls, mistakes and re-dos. Parents do the same in their uncharted quest for the "gold," .....

a child who is curious, social, resilient, self-aware, resourceful, has integrity and is able to wait.

Both my husband and I salute the "greatness" of not only our children, but of our siblings, their spouses and children, and of other relatives and friends. We are proud of all the amazing big successes.... and celebrate the endless small, personal victories. It does "take a village" and we are so grateful for each and every relative and friend "coach" who stood with us on the sidelines of parenting.

The achievements, personalities and honesty of our children, their cousins and friends can only be described as "awesome," as they continue striving to exceed a "personal best." Hats off to all parents who earn endless gold medals surviving "all-nighters" with sick children; suffering tragedy and loss, overcoming disappointing friendships, struggling with difficult career decisions, managing relocation, enduring financial hardships and many, many, many more. There is no Olympic contest with precise training for PARENTING. Most competitors are "ordinary," yet give this job everything they have day after day after day. May every parent accept the olympic challenge of guiding their children to lives of grace. Nothing could be more golden.

"Do What You Love, Love What You Do"

NOW THAT OUR permanent home is located on a northwestern Minnesota lake, my husband and I pick up the weekly local newspaper, to learn about the lives of community neighbors. The stories of hard-working dairy families, Hispanic traditions, local businesses, hometown heroes and children excelling in sports and academics, keep us in touch with local news and issues. We also look forward to the syndicated column of Harvey Mackay, published in a local newspaper. As chairman of MackayMitchell Envelope Company (which Mackay purchased as a small, failing envelope company in 1959 and grew into a $100 million business), Harvey's company philosophy is engrained in the oft-quoted motto: "do what you love, love what you do," with MacKay's addition…and "deliver more than you promise."

Setting aside the authors of the Bible, who are in a category by themselves, another influential writer in the area of human development is Stephen Covey. Covey's book, The 7 Habits of Highly Effective People, defines and actualizes life-building character traits, all underscoring personal integrity. My son gave me this book during his college years and I still refer to Covey's guidelines, attempting application to our marriage, family and all aspects of life…"Be a light, not a judge. Be a model, not a critic. Be part of the solution, not part of the problem."

God, Mackay and Covey share the title of insightful VIP's along with another amazing voice of wisdom. Her title is Mom. She had an uncanny, but natural touch delivered through kind words and positive actions that touched her family and so many others with "lift-up" philosophy and action. When my siblings and I whispered our earthly good-byes to this extremely special human being, who never published a book or wrote a column, we were left with both sorrow and an invaluable gift. Without words, our Mom challenged us to continue life's journey with indelible heart imprints of love and caring for others. Through the life-long language of kindness, commitment and joy in "being," Mom was a role model. My heart will always be filled with gratitude as I savor the brilliance of her ordinary life reflected so gracefully in my sister and sisters-in-law, my daughters and daughter-in-law, my cousins and cousins-in-law, my granddaughters, and my nieces and nieces-in-law. My children's generation exhibits more and more of mom's relational and care-giving qualities, becoming increasingly evident in both the young women and men I have come to know.

Another illuminating story from columnist Ben Holden, published in one of Harvey's columns, focused on doing the 'right thing'........ a new company salesman wrote: "Dear Bos: I have seen this outfit which ain't never bot a dimes worth of nothin from us, and I sole them a couple hundred thousand dollars of guds. I am now going to Chicawgo."

Before the literacy-challenged salesman could be given the heave-ho by the sales manager, this letter came from Chicago: "I cum hear and sole them half a millyon." Fearful of what would happen if he did or did not fire the salesman, the sales manager dumped the problem on the president. The following morning both letters were posted on the bulletin board with the following memo from the president: "To All Salspeople: We ben spending two much time trying to spel instead of trying to sel. Let's watch those sails. I want everybody shud reed these letters from Gooch, who is on the rode doin a grate job for us, and you shud go out and do like he done."   Through both word and action, Mackay advises his readers to 'Swim with the Sharks' (one of his best sellers), without sacrificing personal integrity or doing it at the expense of other people. McKay stressed the importance of personal touch. No question…my mom "mothered" among the best.

Mother, grandmother, great-grandmother, sister, aunt, woman, wife, loved by many, Kathryn did what she loved, loved what she did and delivered, in her meaningful 89 years, so much more than she ever promised. She achieved her GED in her 60's and achieved numerous awards as a leader in 4-H, school activities, church and the Thursday Household Science Club. She never authored a book or made a 6 figure income, but Kathryn did change a "shark" or two. Kathryn, mother of five, grandmother of eleven, set the standard for incomparable delivery of human kindness.

Happily Ever After

"SUCCESS" IS ONE of the biggest, most broadly defined words in the English language. Life skills success often defines the work we do and "relational success" underscores emotional intelligence, utilizing different skills like communication, relationship building and creativity. Two of our grandsons have endured 30 day journeys portaging, paddling and persevering on canoe trips in the Canadian Boundary Waters, mapping their way through unpopulated territory. Their stories are underscored by difficult, challenging experiences and mandated a broad range of technical expertise, creative problem solving, team building, compromise and shared leadership. Survival skills were tested as they endured one challenge after the other to complete their successful journey.

From day one of Mom and Dad's marriage, I think all of Mom's talents, skills and proficiencies were tested, as her newly acquired, no-nonsense mother-in-law taught her the basics of cooking, laundry, housecleaning, gardening, shopping, sewing, and eventually caring for an infant and parenting. She also had to develop skill in butchering, driving a tractor, and assisting with caring for livestock. Was John U, her father-in-law, the teacher? How in the world did this sweet, pampered young 16 year old survive in the uncharted role of teen-age homemaker? She came to this unplanned marriage with skill in making lemonade and brownies. She eventually closed the book on a 73 year marriage as an undeniable expert in every aspect of farm wife and parent. Her "soft skills" made her one of the kindest, most lovable women in Edgar County, where no one had an unkind thought or uttered a negative word about her.

Dad's high school dreams of being a basketball coach took a sharp turn after the "oops!" pregnancy forced his attention to a lifetime of farming. I remember Dad being handy for most of his life with farm equipment, cars, trucks, lawnmowers, barn and household repairs. As I look at young dads today with amazing willingness to cook, change a diaper, grocery shop, clean or do laundry, I am aware that Dad missed that boat. One humorous example was the morning nephew Tim arrived at Mom and Dad's to check on "Grampa." Gramma was in the hospital recuperating from surgery and Dad offered to make coffee for he and Tim. He put water in the pot and dumped the coffee grounds in the water....boiled the coffee....and drank it. As the story goes, Tim politely declined coffee that morning!

At another juncture, Dad seemed to need help in putting on his socks. Mom took on that role in addition to everything else and did it without complaint. One morning when my husband and I were visiting Mom and Dad, my sister arrived to take Mom and I on a little shopping excursion. We had "flown the coop" before Dad realized that he didn't have his socks on yet. He beseechingly looked at my husband and said "Graaaaaama forgot to put my socks on!" His son-in-law respectfully replied, "I don't do socks." Dad pulled on his socks and off they went to check on nuts and bolts in Ashland.

Dad would have scoffed at the term "emotional intelligence." I don't think he saw ANY value in taking vacations and commiserated about the cost. I believe our two vacations growing up had more to do with obligatory reasons (to visit his sister in Texas and a reluctant agreement to join their best friends, Harold and Genevieve on a trip to the Great Smoky Mountains). His disgruntled view of the value of "play" continued into his grandparenting years, when he (probably, reluctantly) agreed to join my siblings and I with all of our children for a week in the beautiful cabins at Boyd's Lodge in Minnesota. As he sat in the rocker on the porch of his cabin, observing the boats and skiers, swimmers, turtle races and outdoor grilling, he remarked,

HAPPILY EVER AFTER

"I never spent so much money doing nothing in my whole life!" As if to make his point, he endured "vacation," wearing his comfortable uniform.... faded bib overalls.

Probably without discussion, Mom and Dad figured out along the way, that their partnership worked. Dad spent most of his life proving to all of the naysayers that he and his "Hambone" (such an adorable nickname) had what it took to "make it!" In fact, he did have the last word on their 73 year marriage as death drew near.... "we showed 'em!"

Kathryn and Ulysses Grant Wright

I Pledge My Head…

LOSING AT SOMETHING can be tough, whether you are a child or an adult. Winning may be accompanied by a ribbon, a medal, trophy or financial reward. I earned a boxful of red, white, blue award ribbons during my 8 years of 4-H and county and state fair exhibits, a couple of purple grand champion ribbons in the food division and two Future Homemaker trophies. In childhood sports competitions such as the annual spring Unit Four Track Meet, I was usually dead last in broad jump, 100 yard dash and pole vault (third grade). I didn't make the High School Varsity Cheerleading Squad. When the May Fete, Tiger Relay and Homecoming Queens were announced, I was honored to be part of their courts. I, however, did not receive an invitation to join the exclusive "girls only" social club. My rejections extended into adulthood. I was runner-up for several Principal and Assistant Principal positions and Community Education Director. I will never forget being called into the Superintendent's office on a particularly devastating occasion where I was demoted from a supervisory position to a program coordinator for unclear reasons. I was stripped of my supervisory responsibilities a day before Christmas Break, assigned to a different building and told to report after January 1 to an administrator who was young, inexperienced and "cute as a button." During Christmas Break, that Superintendent resigned and an interim Superintendent, with whom I had worked extensively, called me to say "you are not going anywhere," and headed me down a much better, more well-suited leadership path.

Losing was tough, but in the process, I experienced a variety of lessons, including not-so-gentle doses of reality. In most contests there is one winner. Losing when I was young, didn't make me feel good, but it didn't paralyze me from trying again to win down the line. I learned how to applaud the achievements of others and swallow my own disappointment. I learned to say "good game," "well done," or "congratulations" and mean it, always bouncing back from my own losses. In the long run, losing was motivational...figuring out how to be smarter, work harder and push the envelope further in the battles I really wanted to win. Eventually the reward for personal effort seldom focused on winning for myself, but on a "win" for the team...a community....a larger cause.

On those occasions when extraordinary effort was rewarded with public acknowledgement and appreciation, I have to admit, it felt pretty darn good! Perhaps my favorite "win" was receiving a Chamber of Commerce award for improving area business climate. The award was given annually to a woman who engaged businesses, organizations, schools and community members in an effort to benefit local businesses. The challenge of rallying the community to restore a boarded up historical theatre in our downtown, was handed to the chair of the newly formed city Arts Commission by the current Mayor. I was that chair. It took nine years, eight million dollars and the collective ingenuity of an amazing group of business leaders and community members, but the doors which originally opened on Christmas Eve, 1921, reopened once again in 2000 as the cultural centerpiece in downtown. The intern involved with the project, who became the renovated Theatre's first director submitted my name for the CC Award. The award came with an invitation to speak at the Annual Chamber Business Awards Luncheon, a corsage, a video highlighting 9 years of meetings and fundraising, and a proud family beaming from the front table, as I approached the podium.

The "win" came with a humbling opportunity to talk about teamwork. My remarks drew upon the 4-H Pledge I learned as a 10-year-old, acknowledging the challenge of keeping committee energy alive for the long-term theatre project. The award belonged to our community, the business men and women who stepped forward to help and my own family and friends who encouraged completion of this important project. I related the Pledge to business success....

In 4-H, we pledged our heads to clearer thinking...underscoring the importance of lifelong learning. Today, "clearer thinking" includes listening to others without a zillion thoughts on one's own mind, understanding the perspectives and realities of others, opening one's mind to new ideas and finding inspiration and insight through clear thinking that remains calm and nonjudgmental. Clear thought also embraces the importance of collaboration. An interdependence on one another is crucial if today's communities are going to be successful in the resolution of challenges. One of my first lessons in the importance of support occurred with the loss of 300 baby chicks, frightened into a corner of suffocation by an owl trapped in a window. It was a monstrous loss for an 11 year old to accept. It was the beginning of an understanding that fear can destroy, but you can't let it be the winner. Life's traumas don't have to be resolved alone.

In 4-H, we pledged our hearts to greater loyalty. Loyalty lessons came in large doses during those 4-H years, in the form of accepting the responsibility of chores, commitments and helpfulness. In addition to chickens, I was responsible for the care of pigs and cattle, learning to sew, cook, garden and arrange flowers. My mom had a lovely way of saying, honey, that zipper isn't quite right, we'd better do it again....or monitoring the positioning of each green bean perfectly aligned in the canning jar to display at the County Fair. My dad did not hesitate saying, "your friends can wait, but the cows don't like sleeping on a wet, soiled bed any better than you would; when the barn is clean and the animals are fed and watered....then you can play...you need to push the work...don't let the work push you!" Loyalty grew out of understanding commitment and responsibility and knowing in my heart that giving up wasn't an option.

A vivid lesson in commitment came the day I was showing my Hampshire pig, Petunia, at the County Fair. As a 13 year old, I was herding a 300 pound sow around the show ring with a dozen other young 4-Hers and saw the judge approach my pig for a better look. I stood straight and tall holding my plywood herding board between me and the pig, lifting the board so that the judge would not be distracted by "too much of me." At that point, the pig's full bladder could wait no more, and Petunia proceeded to drench my little white tennis shoes. When I say the memory was a warm one, it literally was... from my red face to my soaked feet. Sometimes with individual colleagues and in committees, when I think I can't handle any more discussion, any more conflict, any more delay, any more sidetracks, I think of Petunia and know that a "blue ribbon" awaits when the best in all of us comes together in a spirt of "we can do this!" It took 9 years of meetings, hundreds of phone calls and fund-raising visits, along with compromising decisions of many players to reopen the doors of the ruined, water-logged, fire-damaged Paramount, but what a gift at the end of the road!

 We pledged our hands, as 4-Hers, to "larger service" and learned the joy of working together to make things better for someone besides ourselves. There was a lot of competition in 4-H, but it focused on increasing our skills and improving our talents. We grew as a team learning new skills in growing vegetables or raising animals, baking bread or conserving the soil. We learned to face a group and speak and how to sing and perform with confidence. We were expected to carry those skills into our adult lives. The most rewarding part of my life's work has been spent connecting people and their talents to the issues and challenges that come with preparing the next generation to lead meaningful, productive and caring lives. I could not be more proud of the daily efforts that occur in our community schools. The staff throughout our community schools provide a level of loyalty and service to children that is unsurpassed....and it only grows as expectations and responsibilities increase exponentially for our schools. It is essential that business leaders become school partners.

 Finally, we pledged our health to better living....and as an adolescent, I was focused on the physical part. I did place third in the pole vault competition at the Spring Grade School Track Meet. The fact that I was a third grader and there were only three entrants didn't seem particularly significant. A much greater awareness and appreciation of mental fitness has only come in recent years when I have come to understand what 19th Century Lebanese Poet, Kahlil Gibran calls "life's most inmost secret." If you do not love what you do and do what you do not love, you have chosen mundane over music. If I have contributed something to the extraordinary women and men with whom I was privileged to work, it was my desire and ambition to connect them in some way with work they love. I share Gibran's belief that when you are born into the world, your work is born with you. I was born to be an educator and the desire for that work has been in my heart from the moment I arrived. In all parts of my life…right down to my grandchildren…I will strive to search for ways that help others find life "fitness" through meaningful work and greater service.

There are so many people in our community deeply deserving of recognition for thinking clearly, demonstrating loyalty, providing service and building respectful relationships. I challenged Chamber members that day to recognize someone for the gifts they bring to our community. As a follow-up, I asked them to repeat that assignment daily for the rest of their lives so that every member of our community might share the extraordinarily awesome feeling that was bursting inside of me that day!

In the end, it's not about the trophy. It's about learning that winning or losing is simply a state of transience. It never lasts. We win some….we lose some. Winning is merely a marker of "great" in a particular moment. Losing is a reminder that we all have strengths and weaknesses and no one wins all the time. Hundreds of participation ribbons and trophies end up taking up a lot of space, collecting dust on shelves, acknowledging simply that "you showed up" and end up in a box in your parents' house when you move on. Perhaps, the greatest trophies in our collections are memories of the smiles and good feelings resulting from something we have said or done to make someone's life a little better…..no shelf space required!

Here Comes the Sun

I Can See Clearly Now

WE STARTED TODAY viewing the funeral service of the 41st President of the United States. It was very moving as each family member and longtime friend spoke of George Herbert Walker Bush and his legacy. Former Senator Al Simpson offered memorable quotes about our 41st President. He stated that his friend, George Bush, never lost his sense of humor, suggesting that "humor is the universal solvent against the abrasive elements of life." Their mothers instilled a wisdom that both shared..."hatred corrodes the container it's carried in."

Former Canadian Prime Minister Brian Mulroney told the story of walking with Bush to the side of his house at Walker's Point and looking at a small plaque that had been recently installed. It read "CAVU." Bush explained that the letters stood for "Ceiling and visibility unlimited," a reference to the words he hoped to hear before takeoff as a young pilot in the pacific. It meant perfect flying and it was Bush's way of describing a perfect life with friendships at the heart of his blessed life. Prime Minister Mulroney offered this poem:

> There are wooden ships,
> There are sailing ships,
> There are ships that sail the sea,
> But the best ships are friendships
> And may they always be.

The fate of one's life rests in God's hands, but He continues to provide opportunities along the way and leaves the choice in our hands. The slate is blank at birth and when God has a plan that challenges us, or tears us apart or leaves us with a daunting "why," we are often angry and dismissive of the God who promises to "keep us always in his care."

One of my favorite stories about how we "color" life's journey is about a couple of men in residence at a hospital, both seriously ill. They shared a small room with one window. One of the men, as part of his treatment, was allowed to sit up in bed for an hour in the afternoon in order to drain the fluid from his lungs. His bed was next to the window. The other man had to spend all of his time flat on his back. Every afternoon when the man next to the window was propped up for his hour, he would pass the time by describing what he could see outside. The window apparently overlooked a river and a park. There were ducks and geese in the river, children came to throw bread and families played and had picnics in the park and because it was fall, the trees were resplendent in their glorious colors. The man on his back would listen to the other man describe all of this, enjoying every minute. He heard about the frisbee that flew into the lake, the softball games and the children playing on the swings and slides. His friend's descriptions eventually made him feel he could almost see what was happening outside. One afternoon, the thought struck him. Why should the man next to the window have all the pleasure of seeing what was going on? Why shouldn't he get the chance? He felt ashamed, but the more he tried not to think like that, the worse he wanted a change! Eventually, the man next to the window passed away and his roommate asked if he could be switched to the bed next to the window. So they moved him, tucked him in and made him quite comfortable. The minute they left, he propped himself up on one elbow, painfully and laboriously, and looked out the window. It faced a blank wall.

God does have a vision for each life that, more often than not, is invisible. He equips us with capacity for change and adaptation. Our children, their children and every one of God's children require broad strokes of encouragement, kindness and direction in order to achieve joyful, fulfilled lives. The "Greatest Generation" did not end with World War II. The potential for "greatness" exists in all generations, when serious attention is devoted to the development of those who follow. Fostering growth, friendships, each other's well-being and honest respect for all people….in schools, businesses, organizations, church….and up and down the street will frame a world with love, happiness and grace. Former President George Herbert Walker Bush's CATV parallels God's hope for humanity…"ceiling and visibility unlimited." When humans are able to see beyond self-imposed "walls," we will be ready for take-off!

You can't go back and change the beginning, but you can start where you are and change the ending. C.S. Lewis

Marriage#Trust

55 YEARS OF Marriage#??.....hmmm, what should the hashtag be.... what is the theme....what is the crux....is there a legacy....what word should I use to characterize the prose and poetry of our 55 year marriage? Some thoughts come to mind.... PRIORITY....FAITH... COURAGE.....DETERMINATION.

My memories drift to a beautiful, warm, sunny day more than a decade ago in the Tuscan Hills of Italy. Relaxing on the patio of a repurposed quaint villa, surrounded by the scents of olive trees and grape vineyards, my husband and I waited for the church bells to chime. Soon, the bells began to ring, signaling the arrival of the local Priest and summoning those within hearing distance to Sunday morning Mass. We walked the short distance to the large, old stone edifice with our daughter, son-in-law and 18 month old granddaughter on a beautiful fall day in October, 2006. We entered the church's gigantic wooden doors and quietly slipped into the plain wooden pews. Father Domenic slowly shuffled into the sacristy, supported precariously by the straight back of a wooden chair. The Priest's faltering arrival immediately lowered our level of concern about keeping a curious 18 month old quiet for the duration of the Mass. It was sure to be short! And in the beautiful language of our host country and the Roman Catholic Church, Father Domenic proceeded to recite familiar prayers. With the ancient salutation, "Dominus Nobiscum," he invited God to be with us as we celebrated Mass with our neighbors across the ocean. Father Dominic's voice resonated throughout the lofty church to the 19 parishioners in attendance. Prayers were ancient and brief. Good, so far! The Homily was certain to be quick, given Father's apparently unstable physical condition. At the appropriate time, Father slowly turned the chair toward the handful of the faithful, creeped around it and sat down. For the next forty-five minutes, the church vibrated with the intensity, passion and fervor of a message that resounded, "THIS IS A PRIORITY!" In a foreign language unknown to us, two words literally bounced off the walls and drilled deep. The Priest's booming voice and energetic delivery belied our previous misconceptions about his "state of health" and the PRIORITY of "matrimonium" and "familia" was resoundingly clear! Even our tiny granddaughter was captivated by the Priest's booming respect for the sacrament of marriage, a story I look forward to sharing on her wedding day. Marriage, according to Father Dominic was…is…and shall remain a PRIORITY….and always in the context of reverence for family. Marriage#PRIORITY!

And there is FAITH. Stories abound about our respective ancestors and I am especially grateful to my husband's Aunts Leora and Lucy, and to my sister and her daughter for pursuing the histories of our families. My husband's English ancestry has been traced by Hawkins descendants back to Sir John Hawkins who served England between the mid 1500's and his death in 1595. Sir John was an English slave trader, naval commander and administrator, merchant, navigator, shipbuilder and privateer. His infamous history includes treasure-hunting in the West Indies, fighting against the Spanish Armada, slave trade and plotting to assassinate Elizabeth I. Sir John and his cousin Sir Frances Drake were considered brave explorers who led the way to America for the early colonists…..and now I have a clue about where my husband's "risk-taking, visionary" genes originated!!

Another intriguing story of courage and faith began in 1720 with the birth of Robert Headley, my mother's ancestor and one of eight children. Robert was living in Wyoming Valley, Pennsylvania just prior to the historical massacre of the settlers in that location, near Headleytown (now Uniontown). Robert had taken care of a native

Indian through a severe illness. Just prior to the massacre, the native warned Robert to take his family and leave the valley immediately, which he did. Colonel Butler, a renegade Torie, had offered easy surrender terms and induced settlers who had taken refuge in the Pennsylvania fort to return to their homes. On July 4th, Colonel Butler, with his band of Tories and Indians, returned to Wyoming Valley and massacred everyone in the settlement. Only because of the warning of a grateful Indian was the Headley branch of the family saved to posterity. Faith in humankind led Robert to load his family in a canoe and leave his home upon a moment's notice under the darkness of night!

Turning the calendar to barely more than a century earlier, I contemplated the significance of COURAGE in my husband's Marchetti ancestors. In 1886, a teen-aged girl, Domenica Dellaca and her parents, Catherine and John, along with two sisters, departed from their Italian home and sailed to America in hopes of a better life. Lorenze Marchetti arrived at Ellis Island on the same ship, the first vessel of immigrants to be welcomed by the newly commissioned and open arms of the Statue of Liberty. Lorenze, Domenica and her family waited patiently to be cleared as immigrants from Cuasolo and Turine, Italy, eager to begin a life full of promise in the United States of America. They gave up everything, including the Italian spelling of their surname, Marchetti, because the American gatekeepers could spell and more accurately pronounce Marketto.

Domenica and Lorenze were married in Indiana and gave birth to 13 children, eleven of whom survived. One of those 11, Norma Frances, was mom to my husband. His grandparents made the foreboding decision to seek a better life in America, leaving behind all that they knew and loved. Their entire life stories were fueled by COURAGE. Young, inexperienced, heading to a culture where the language and the customs were unknown, there were no jobs waiting; there were no family or friends; there was no place to stay or familiar food to eat, but they had the COURAGE to believe that they would find their way. And they did, enjoying long, productive lives, raising 11 of their 13 children to adulthood and creating a safe, fulfilling life for their family. The Italian immigrants were dedicated to a strong faith in God, marriage and family as they established roots and made contributions in America's small mining communities. Marriage# COURAGE.

Subsequently, I considered a marriage underscored by DETERMINATION! On July 7, 2009, my parents, Kathryn Jane and Ulysses Grant celebrated their final wedding anniversary together, honoring 72 years of marriage. Pregnant and unmarried at 15, mom and dad (19) had no alternative but to give their newborn son up for adoption. Mom returned to Illinois from her "flu recovery" at a home for unwed mothers in Kansas City, MO under a parental threat that "the scoundrel responsible would be sent to the penitentiary if he ever came near their daughter again." In a couple of months, the young couple eloped! From that moment on, my parents' mantra was DETERMINATION. We will show them! And through the trials of giving up their firstborn, followed by the death of Martha, their two-year-old second-born to Peritonitis after swallowing a piece of glass, they bravely faced each day. Life's storms continued through droughts, hail storms, unforgiving parents, unstable grain and livestock prices and the challenges of raising three subsequent children. In spite of personal losses, coupled with the slow economic recovery following World War II and the Great Depression, they persevered. They found a marital rhythm built on very clear roles, hard work and shared values. They vowed that "their marriage would not fail." In the last moments of final interaction with my 93 year old Dad, in a weakened frail state, he glared at me and declared, "We showed 'em!" I have no doubt about the meaning behind those words. Mom's determination was woven carefully and continuously among her kind thoughts, deeds and loving attention to her family and all who knew her. She was determined to care for her family as long as she could breathe and in the last conversation I had with her the night she died, six months after Dad's passing, I asked her if she was ready to "be with dad?" She replied with a sleepy grin, "not quite yet!" Her family still needed her…and she was right! But Dad undoubtedly pestered God relentlessly to call Mom home and God finally gave in. Marriage# DETERMINATION.

So, our own 50th anniversary milestone has come and gone. What defines my husband and I, underscoring our journey as a married couple? Our faith is real and we discover our spirituality in meaningful ways as we grow older. We like accomplishing things. We are unbelievably proud of the children we created and for whom, my husband likes to suggest "we will never complete a touchdown." Our children, grandchildren, siblings, extended family and friends bring us more joy than we could have ever imagined….and we anticipate more to come. We do not expect to become old "in spirit." We want to keep learning and growing. We try to be thoughtful about our health, our security, mental well-being and our world. We like each other and enjoy spending time together even though our interests often take us in different directions.

Our marriage has had ups and downs, but underlying those highs and lows is our hashtag…a deep and enduring TRUST. That's OUR word. Reminding ourselves that working to make each other the "best we each can be" enhances the development, strengthening, and permanency of a strong and supportive marriage. The love of family flavors this marriage, which started hesitantly 50 years ago with a stuttered "I do," and continues to overflow with God's blessings every day of our union. Without a shadow of doubt, my husband and I trust that we can count on God, assisted by each other and those we love, throughout the twists and turns of life until "death do us part." Marriage# TRUST.

MARRIAGE#TRUST

Marjorie and Garry

Deceased Diva

NOW... A REFLECTION on probably the most embarrassing thing I ever did. During my early years in the local public School District, media services were provided to all of the elementary and secondary schools from a central building. Everyone loved the guy who transported the overhead projectors, the movie projectors, slide projectors, stand-alone movie screens and assorted light bulbs to schools as they needed them. Of course, our eight elementary schools and four secondary schools did not have their own equipment....can you even imagine??? The media equipment van driver's name was Al....I don't think many people knew his last name....we always referred to him as "Al from Media." He had a great personality and everyone loved him. When Al was in his 60's, we shared his sadness at the loss of his wife due to a long term illness.

Later that week, I wanted to pay my respects to Al and headed to the funeral home to share my sympathy. When I arrived, there were two deceased ladies in two different rooms, and I realized I did not know Al's last name. I made my best guess and walked into the first room, instantly aware that, other than the guy sitting in the front row, I was the only person in the room with the deceased. I recognized Al from the back (or so I thought), and confidently walked forward, feeling so glad that I had come since no one else was there to share his grief.

When I got to the casket, I realized that the woman was much older than Al's wife would have been and the man sitting about three steps behind me was not Al. I stood there thinking, OMG, what can I say to the only relative/friend in the room!!!! What if he wants to talk about his "loved one?" I was desperately trying to figure out a way to make a graceful exit...when, sure enough....he got up and walked over to stand beside me. I stammered, "she looks so lovely in that beautiful dress," (a lacy black and gold sparkly party gown that I can still visualize) and he replied, "she wore that dress when she was married." We managed to continue the conversation a bit longer as I prayed that another visitor would take my place. No such luck, and then he asked, "and how did you know my mother?" I had no idea how long they had lived in the community or, if in fact, they even lived in the community. I just softly said, "oh, our paths crossed a long time ago...I am so sorry for your loss, and I must go now and visit the other family here this evening"...and I fled before he could say more. He may still be wondering who in the world was that woman???

I found Al in the next room, which was filled with colleagues and family. Al proudly introduced me to his two grandsons. Months later, when Al and I were reflecting on his wife's absence from his life, he shared that he had not seen his grandsons for five years prior to her death! He had been estranged from these young grandsons for most of their lives and did not know where they had disappeared to with their mother, Al's daughter-in-law! My mouth dropped open and I told an astonished Al that the boys were no strangers to me....they played in our back yard often because their other grandparents lived across the alley and they visited those grandparents often. Truth is stranger than fiction! Al "took the bull by the horns," and was able to reconcile with his grandsons and daughter-in-law who lived in a different school district only a few miles away.

I loved telling the story of the "deceased Diva!" Several years later, after Al had retired from the School District, I was reconstructing my embarrassing encounter during an evening out in a local restaurant with a group of friends. Amid much laughter (at my expense), I did not realize that there was another group listening to my story. When they left the restaurant, they stopped by the table and

FATHER, MAY I...

laughingly explained, they had also known Al and loved hearing him "brought to life" again.

So, all of life's events—good, bad, and embarrassing, teach us something. I have often wished that I had admitted to the mystery man that "I had made a mistake, but, while I am here, tell me a little about your mother and your life together....."

Hello?

"HELLO?" I ANSWERED on the turquoise wall phone during an August evening in my family's home August 5, 1966. A long-distance operator asked if Esther Gilbert were available. Startled for a moment, I replied, "Esther Gilbert is long deceased, but her husband (my grandfather) is here if you would like to talk with him. The caller responded, "No."

A bit later, my Aunt Gerry answered a second phone call with a boisterous "hello!" This time, the operator asked for U.G. Wright. "Yeah, he's here….just a minute…." Aunt Gerry yelled up the stairs where Dad had just retired, "U.G., phone for you!" Story telling resumed in the kitchen with extended family members who had just shared my wedding rehearsal dinner in a near-by town.

Within minutes, my Dad called down the stairs for "Hambone," an unusual nickname bestowed upon my mother, Kathryn, long ago by her spouse. As she entered their bedroom, Dad sat upright in their bed, looked incredulously at my Mother and whispered emotionally, "After all these years of searching for our son, God has led him to us!"

Dad handed the phone to Mom. Years after cradling her newborn baby for a few illegal moments far from home, a quivering Kathryn cradled a telephone receiver that would leap over the past 29 years in about as many seconds. Unforgettable scenes raced through her mind as the phone rang twice …..an explosion of memories….the silent ride with furious parents across two state borders... abandonment at the Willows Maternity Sanitarium for Unwed Mothers in Kansas City,

FATHER, MAY I...

Missouri.... the tearful good-bye to her newborn son and the loneliness of 3 months away from home and family, allegedly overcoing a "serious case of the flu." A few days after "the flu" was cured, Mom's parents retrieved their daughter and drove home in stony silence....determined to return their daughter to normal teen high school life. The return-to-normal directive was frequently underscored by the warning, "if that scum gets anywhere close to you again, we will see that he is sent to the Penitentiary!"

Days after arriving home in central Illinois in April, 1937, 16 year old Kathryn Gilbert and 20 year old U.G. Wright drove to a nearby town, falsified Mother's age on the marriage certificate and pledged their lives to one another for better or worse. Unfortunately, "worse" got underway the next morning when their marriage was reported in the area newspaper. A prominent family began to crumble under the raised eyebrows of reputation scandal!

Unbeknownst to me, in 1966, as I was packing my bag for a week's honeymoon, Mom and Dad were confiding quietly, making plans for a trip to Oklahoma to meet their son. The existence of a fifth sibling in our family had been kept secret from their other children. Mom and Dad painfully held their breaths one more week until my home-grown brother's wedding, seven days after mine.

Two weddings down....a long road trip from Illinois to Oklahoma.....heart rates off the chart.....a knock on the door of a strange house in a strange city.....prayers were answered and there he was, the spittin' image of his birth father. Well, hello......

The "Good" in "Good-Bye"

TONIGHT WE TIGHTLY hugged our beautiful granddaughter, as we expressed positive wishes for a college journey that begins tomorrow when her whole family heads to South Dakota State University for a ten o'clock "move-in." Hannah is so excited, so well prepared and so ready for this next big step in defining her life. How could we not be happy for this day.....for this turn in the road....for this beautiful human being on the threshold of a future without boundaries?

I am feeling a little guilty as I remember my own start to college as kind of a non event. I was excited about learning....not so much about moving away from home, making new friends and heaven-forbid, "rabble rousing!" I don't remember an emotional tug-of-war or a tearful departure. On the other hand, when my own children happily approached the milestones of Kindergarten, High School, College, Marriage, Babies and Careers, my mind celebrated, but my heart needed a wheelbarrow. Was Mom sad...did she feel a loss when I left the nest? I know she was proud, but I don't remember talking to her about how she felt. With whom did she share her joys and heartaches? Maybe Mom and Dad were well trained at hiding their sorrows...they certainly had many opportunities to practice. Maybe because I was only 30 miles away at college....maybe, because I had to drive to Indiana State those first couple of weeks since housing was granted first to in-state students...maybe because I wasn't the first child to leave home....maybe I was so focused on the exciting journey ahead of me, I didn't see the pain that I believe

FATHER, MAY I...

is inevitable when one person in any relationship moves on and the other stays behind.

Dad bought a used pea-green Ford for me to drive those first two weeks of college. I stayed overnight with Susie, the friend who introduced me to Garry five years earlier, until the very old Knisely Apartments were opened to "overflow" students. Eight girls sharing a bathroom was not fun! One of my roommates delighted in rushing into the common bathroom and flushing the toilet while you were still using it! Garry and I began dating again soon after I started school at ISU, so most of my visits home were not alone. In hindsight, I wish I could rewrite my awareness of what really mattered to people I loved. I work hard at that today.

I anticipated that our wedding and departure for Minnesota "milestones" would be tough ones, but everything turned upside down with Richard's phone call on the eve of our wedding. I didn't quite understand the "aura" during the back to back weddings of myself and John. But with a week to go before Garry and I left "home" for new jobs, new challenges and the beginning of a new marriage, the answer unfolded. Knowing that they would be gone during our own departure to Minnesota, Mom, Dad, Patti and Grandmother Nichols headed for Oklahoma and the wildly anticipated reunion with my parents' first-born child. My parents "good-bye" was loaded with distraction and emotion that I could certainly rationalize....but still!!! We spent our final week with Garry's family, followed by two hundred miles of tears and sadness as we drove away from all that we knew and loved. However, a state trooper "turned on the red—get sensible now—light" and pulled our car over, ready to impound all of our worldly possessions in our 5X7 U-Haul trailer with expired license plates. Then, after the U-Haul side mirrors fell off the car and we ran over them, our journey led us to Madison, Wisconsin. The discovery of Denny and Mary Lou Adams, long-time friends from my hometown (also staying at the Howard Johnson Hotel) helped us take a deep breath and calmly continue our journey to Minnesota the next morning.

I have good, positive memories of hitting my own milestones of graduations, achievements, marriage, babies and careers. I was proud to celebrate the milestones of my siblings (cheerleading, homecoming queen, basketball, Eastern Illinois University, Washington University Dental School, marriages, babies and careers). We all were moving on…and I didn't dwell on whom we were leaving behind. Ouch!

But, it's never too late. Self-help books remind me that happiness depends upon successful living "in the moment," savoring and enjoying the amazing opportunities, experiences and relationships that grace the lives of our children, grandchildren, siblings and their families and friends. Being "in the moment" lets go of past mistakes, avoids worries of the future and allows me to appreciate all of God's little treasures along the way. So I am relishing being in the moment as Hannah prepares to walk through an amazing door. I love the joy of this moment that fills me with, not sorrow, but gratitude….even though a little tear slides down gramma's cheek.

Through the Years...
with Brothers

BROTHERS CAN BE pesky growing up, but the older I get, the more I appreciate the fact that I was privileged to have two brothers who couldn't be more different, yet both warm and fill my soul with gratitude.

John Henry loved to play pranks and enjoyed even more, laughing when the pranks were successfully carried off. He hid around corners, under beds, in our closet, behind trees, in barns, in the outhouse, in the haymow... just waiting for the next opportunity to jump out and scare his sisters. Of course, his most famous "scare" occurred one evening when my "date" got in his car and drove out the farm driveway on his way back home to Terre Haute. John had climbed into the back seat, and jumped up, grabbing my future husband by the shoulders and emitting a Tarzan yell! Thank goodness, there was no heart attack or car wreck! To this day, John continues to relish teasing his sisters, "twisting the meaning" of most everything, seeking a humorous reaction to most interactions. Almost every comment is accompanied by a chuckle and a wry grin. I do think he looks at the glass "half-full!" John carries a tremendous love in his heart for all of his family and is sincerely dedicated to their well-being. He is a Shepherd in every sense of the word, savoring God's word and expressing gratitude for His gifts of family and the land. John leads with our mother's kindness, our dad's dedication to family and God's Word.

THROUGH THE YEARS...WITH BROTHERS

When I think of memories with John, I think of...... Unit Four Orphans and Paris Tiger Basketball...Sunrise Little League Baseball...Multiflora Rose Bushes around the pond...Erector Sets...Monopoly...Pit...miniature tractors and road graders in the sand pile...red convertible...Joey Chitwood Performances on our Bicycles...railroad track on his bedroom floor...Cowboys, Indians, and BB guns...4-H Tours and North Arm Hustlers...haymow tunnels...Hedge Apple trees...and the outrageous cost of 7-Up in St. Louis, where we celebrated his graduation from Dental School.

I will always share with my brother, John, the memory of our "date" in 1957 with our grandmother and step-grandfather. I wore my yellow dotted Swiss dress to the Terre Haute Country Club Youth Dance and John was in sports jacket and tie. I was an 8th grader and John was a freshman. Mary Fread clip clopped across the patio tile floor in very high heels, insisting that John and I join her daughter, Susie, and her junior high friends. We reluctantly acquiesced and a lovely 60 year friendship ensued with Susie, quickly leading to meeting the guy who lived across the alley. A long acquaintance with "that guy" led to marriage with the love of my life nine years later. Much of that journey was shared with my brother, John.

When my older brother (born 29 years earlier) arrived in my life, I had built a mountain of memories in 22 years with John! On the eve of my marriage, Richard Byron, at age 29, located his birth parents (which just so happened to be the same as mine)! Unbeknownst to me, preparations were begun that night for a reunion with a family that Richard had never known and only recently learned about. Over a year later, in late November of 1967, a few days prior to my sister's wedding, Richard, his wife, and three children walked through the back storm door at the farm house for my first interaction with a "new brother!" I genuinely and enthusiastically proclaimed, "Welcome Family!" The days in the short visit were a blur as we prepared for Patti's wedding and celebrated Thanksgiving with an extended family. My biggest first impression was how much he looked like our Dad.

The next couple of decades found all of my siblings busy with

FATHER, MAY I...

raising families, working and catching up at Christmas. Finally with retirement, the gatherings became more intentional and increasingly special as we connected in Paris, Dallas, Montreal and at Little Birch Lake.

John, Marjorie, Richard

The more we had a chance to share stories, dreams and feelings, the more I discovered my new "older brother" and I shared traits of loving one on one conversation, acknowledging feelings and encouraging each other to follow our dreams. One very special occasion where these traits blossomed, occurred in the beautiful fall landscape near Montreal, Canada in October, 2016 when Richard and Marty, John and Marilyn, Greg and Patti and Garry and I gathered to celebrate 50 years of marriage for myself, siblings John and Patti (just one year short) and our spouses. We also celebrated 50 years of welcoming Richard into his birth family. Long walks and heartfelt talks graced the agenda, in the midst of the most spectacular view of fall Canadian colors. We celebrated family with delicious meals, great stories and a hair-raising...."almost didn't make it" ride to catch our plane back to the States.

Richard is a "glass half-full" brother too. He celebrates the good in everyone and is straightforward in expressing his thoughts. The walks are never long enough in Texas, Minnesota, Canada, Arizona or Illinois.

Through the Years... with Sisters

MARTHA JANE WAS my older sister. She was God's gift to a young couple, our mom and dad, born on April 15, 1939. Martha was born two years after they had to leave their first baby in Kansas City, Missouri, eventually to be adopted by a loving family. Mom was 18 and Dad was 22. Martha was the apple of everyone's eye. Her blond curly hair and blue eyes melted the hearts of everyone and soon brought reconciliation between Kathryn and her parents, who had been estranged since the elopement of their daughter and U.G. on July 7, 1937.

Martha Jane died in the Paris Hospital when she was two years old. A couple of days before her death from Peritonitis, she bit into a drinking glass and swallowed enough glass fragments to lacerate the lining of her stomach. I did not know about Martha until I was about 14. I discovered Martha's obituary in a box of old papers in the bathroom closet, to which I was attempting to bring some order. When I approached Mom with a confused set of questions, I got a very brief answer and the case was closed. The newspaper indicated that Martha had died on July 9, 1941 of injuries received when a horse kicked her. Mom and Dad had discovered their two year old sitting in the orchard crying and initially speculated that she had been injured by their horse.

In the days before Mom died at age 89, she confided to Patti that she still carried the guilt of not taking good enough care of Martha. I believe Patti's strong words that day of God's love and forgiveness allowed Mom to finally forgive herself. I remember one very special moment when Mom and I visited the cemetery during our Christmas visit to check on the graves decorated with Christmas wreaths. On Martha's tombstone, a tiny bright red bow peeked out under the freshly fallen snow. My tears were unleashed....no words were needed, but that day a mother and daughter shared a deep, deep unforgotten grief. I was deeply touched by Mom's sharing of that love of Martha on that cold December day.

The loss of Martha led to Mom and Dad's willingness to try for more children, even though their financial situation was very strained. Dad had to sell his recently purchased red truck to pay for Martha's burial. They had very little. On May 19, 1942, John Henry arrived and fifteen months later, Marjorie was born. Three years later, my sister, Patricia rounded out the family. While I have a basketful of memory snippets of our growing up years, they are mostly centered around family meals, preparation of 4-H baking, sewing and animal projects; 4-H meetings; school activities and holiday gatherings on Easter, Thanksgiving and Christmas. Her most annoying habit was taking her tiger-shaped pajama bag to bed each night. The bag contained a small music box that played "Tiger Rag," and she played it over and over in spite of my loud complaints!

Even though Patti and I shared a bedroom for 19 years, the three years difference in our ages limited our personal interactions. We had a little tiny triangle closet in the corner of our room that was more than adequate for the couple of dresses we each had, two pairs of shoes and a couple of blouses and skirts.

Our personalities were different. I was a planner and I liked "orderly." Patti was much more spontaneous and she liked to stir things up a bit. I liked to study and was a project person. Patti met all the requirements for most any task, but quit when she was satisfied that she had done "enough." When it was time to dry the evening supper dishes, I loved putting a smile on Mom's face with a "tinkle, tinkle" appearance of the magic fairy carrying a dish towel. Patti wasn't all that crazy about doing dishes and disappeared into the bathroom to do "her business," and showed up with a dish towel when most of the dishes were back in the cabinets.

My "take" on sports involved competing in the Unit Four spring track meet and cheerleading. Patti was a star in the Girls Athletic Association (GAA). She could play softball with the best of female athletes and win at competitive track events. She was an athletic cheerleader, but declined the opportunity her senior year. Gratitude for my sister's life was immersed in horrific sorrow that year when the high school principal and two of the cheerleaders were killed in a car accident on their way home from an out of town basketball game.

I enjoyed high school participation in Girls Chorus, a Girls Ensemble, Mixed Choir and <u>Tiger Tales</u>, the high school newspaper. Patti sang in high school and is still singing in the First United Methodist Choir. Her performances, both solo and with a variety of friends are first class! Patti sang with a quartet of high school friends called The Four Winds and won first place in a talent competition at the Illinois State Fair, earning the right to sing with pop star, Bobby Vinton.

I am a worrier and tend to think in the future. Patti is a preserver and loves recalling and sharing stories from the past. Her talents in genealogy, family history and stories, and preservation of community history are gifts to her family and many Paris friends and residents. She is a Daughter of the American Revolution and arduous volunteer at the Edgar County Historical Museum and the Edgar County Fair. She has provided respected leadership throughout our hometown's long-established Methodist Church. She is a welcome "force" in the choir loft, in a next door garden, the church council and through Bible Studies. Patti discovers and shares much joy as mom, wife, sister, cousin and friend in pursuit of loving relationships and interactions with family and hometown residents.

We share membership in the Philanthropic Educational Organization. We have always been united in a love of teaching. She connects with children in a meaningful, heartfelt way. From Patti's love for her four kind, loving, resourceful children and seven grandchildren to cousins, nieces, nephews, neighbors, former students and friends, she is a supporter of growth and happiness. From teaching Sunday School... to telling the Sunday children's story... to teaching at Miss Jean's Nursery School...to teaching Head Start...to protecting children through the Department of Children and Family Services...to so many heartfelt and attentive conversations with little people, including her children, nieces and nephews, her joy in making life good for children simply makes her glow.

Patricia and Marjorie

FATHER, MAY I...

    I deeply admire her faith. Patti loves and serves God and shares her faith with all those she meets. My sister lives God's Word every day and it is most evident in her abilities to forgive and lift others up. Patti sees the best in everyone and accepts God's Will with grace and quiet strength. I admire and am grateful for her lifetime of unselfish caregiving for our parents. I also admire the beautiful balanced relationship she shares with her husband, Greg. They both work hard at making each other the best they can be.

    Especially during the past decade, our sisterhood can only be described as radiantly joyful. Our lives intersect meaningfully within the happy, energy-filled chaos of our families. We both strive to immerse our thoughts, wishes and needs in "all that is good" by dancing in the present. We shared a home, a bedroom, a collie, Hunter Calico 4-H, First United Methodist Church, brothers, schools, Mickey Mouse Club, county fairs, homemade noodles, ice cream, caramels and family. Nothing can match the enormity of love for my beautiful sister. I think I could even tolerate a round or two of the "Tiger Rag".....

Don't Stop Believing

Jesus at Michael's

THERE WE WERE....A table of 5 sad, mopey faces, looking at menus and preparing to order our evening meal at Michael's Restaurant in Rochester, Minnesota (c. 2005). With increasing frequency, our family traveled to the Mayo Clinic in Rochester to accompany my husband's sister, Nancy, to doctor visits, cancer-reduction infusions, doctor evaluations and hundreds of tests. Our children all made valiant efforts to share Nancy's journey, and on this particular week-end, her youngest niece and family were living in England. Our two other children were able to occasionally spend time in Rochester, and were there with my husband and I that week-end. There didn't seem to be a lot to be cheerful about and after several years of fighting non-Hodgkins Mantle Cell Lymphoma, Nancy's spirit was taking a dive as the fight dragged on. Those who intentionally and faithfully chose to accompany her on this challenging journey of needles, remissions, relapses and dwindling energy were also feeling the strain.

In our shared grieving, Nancy and her family had drifted toward fear and frustration, questioning the reminder in Psalms 46:1-2, "God is our shelter and strength, always ready to help in times of trouble." God assures us in this psalm... " we will not be afraid, even if the earth is shaken and mountains fall into the ocean depths, even if the seas roar and rage, and the hills are shaken by the violence." Everyone was cancer weary, understanding the relentless progression of Nancy's illness and feeling helpless. So, that evening, in Michael's Restaurant, we made an effort to find "edible diversion" on the large menu.

FATHER, MAY I...

Our young waiter approached the table, and gaily announced, *"Hello! I am Dallas, your server this evening. Do my teeth look ok? I am so embarrassed, but I have a couple of fake teeth in front….they are only temporary, but I am worried that they don't look right. What do you think?"* The giggles started when Dallas went off to get our drinks. Dallas was of slight build and had blond hair that was thin and looked as though it could not be tamed. He had a few scratches on his face, that he pointed out were healing nicely. Dallas returned with our drinks and went on with the story…..he had been visiting friends in St. Paul a couple of weeks ago and had gotten beaten up, and those guys *"knocked my two front teeth out!"* He had just returned to work that day after getting his temporary teeth and was so concerned that he would look or talk funny with teeth that were, of course, going to be replaced with real teeth. *"Well, not real teeth,"* he exclaimed, *"but you know what I mean! Are you ready to order?"*

I have no idea what we ordered for dinner that evening, but Dallas dished up commentary throughout the meal that would have brought the house down at any comedy club. He shared more of his story about the past, present, and future of his teeth. As the evening wore on, the five of us couldn't refrain from the laughter and grins that stirred an amazing healing for all of us. Dallas was enjoying our questions and concerns in an ongoing dialogue and by the time Michael's was ready to close for the evening, Nancy asked for the bill and added a $100 tip for the goofy young man who unknowingly led us away from pain and sadness for a most welcome respite.

When we returned to the hotel, our daughter took a mobile phone down to the end of the hallway and checked in with her husband. As she related what had happened during the dinner at Michael's, our daughter's husband asked quietly with sincere intent, *"are you sure it wasn't Jesus?"*

Our family returned to Michael's Restaurant a few days after the first visit, and asked for Dallas. The wait staff did not remember anyone named Dallas who had worked there. *But…* I'm convinced that Jesus was there. His name, that night, was Dallas.

For I know the plans I have for you, declares the Lord, plans for welfare and not for evil, to give you a future and a hope. Jeremiah 29:11

Flower Whisperer

THERE IS MAGIC in her touch. She whispers words of encouragement to tiny living things that bloom in all colors of the rainbow. She can bring back to life a sad, wilted leaf and restore the beauty of a plant drooping from neglect. She is my friend, Sue....a nurse for green things, a caretaker for beautiful things, a counselor for plants and gardens that make us smile. Sue is a restoration artist for aging things that appear to be wilting or going "over the hill" and a "whisperer," with knowledge and determination skillfully bringing back to life "plants in despair!"

God graced each of His human creations with different gifts. My husband and I were graced with the location of our first apartment as newlyweds in St. Cloud, MN. Two buildings away and two days later, we met Sue, husband Tim and baby Mark. Recently, these forever friends, visited us in the southwest soaking up sunshine, recalling favorite memories and enjoying the comfort of friendship that has brought joy for more than 55 years.

Sue and I have celebrated birthdays, dinners, bridge, card games, child-rearing, homemaking, husband coaching and even a very special trip to Hawaii. But there is one skill where Sue outshines nearly everyone! She has an intuitive sense of what living plants need to flourish. There is a huge, loving capacity in Sue that embraces the well-being of flowers and plants. She quietly assesses their needs and goes to work without directions, a "how-to" pamphlet or a plant blog.

During our recent visit, I watched Sue operate on auto-pilot, as she made a bee-line to patio plants that needed dead-heading and a drink of water. Her vision for "what could be," and her bent, but nimble fingers lovingly performed plant CPR (critical plant resuscitation). Her brain focused on the task, her heart rejoiced and Sue's lips whispered love and admiration to her newest batch of nature's "babies."

Much like a bee, Sue is excited every Spring, ready to celebrate the bright green of new "sprouts" to watch over and enjoy. I am not surprised by her moving lips as she convinces the flowers in her care to be strong, beautiful and fragrant as they reach for the sun.

I believe it is human nature to seek the healing power of the sun and to relish the attention of caretaking. My friend, Sue, "floats her boat" in the soil of thriving plants. I pray that she will always be surrounded by their life-enhancing power. Leaning in closely, I hear prayer in her whispers. I am assured, as mother nature relishes Sue's loving touch, that the warmth of family and the tenderness of plants and flowers will always illuminate her soul. Growing thriving plants can be a challenging task, much like "becoming a senior." Traveling the "road of aging" can also become a daunting journey, as our stems weaken, our bloom fades and life gives way to the "young." I seek to share Sue's soft-spoken words of encouragement with all of humanity..."get rid of the weeds that drag you down, stimulate growth in your life through people and environments that you enjoy and whisper frequently to the Master Gardener, who promises the beauty of eternal life."

Lookin' for Love in all the Wrong Places

EARLY MEMORIES OF my Dad paint a picture of my siblings sitting in the back of a wagon, pulled by two work horses named Shorty and Bell. We regularly hopped off the wagon to open and shut wooden gates as we accompanied Mom and Dad completing farm chores. We all had a role in filling feed troughs and water tanks for farm animals, picking persimmons, burning trash, cleaning out barns, throwing shelled corn for the pheasants, picking up sticks, planting and harvesting garden produce and laying down fresh straw in animal beds.

Work hard...clean up your plate....there are starving children in China...work before play...help your neighbors...do what's right. And.don't give money through church for Zimbabwe natives to build a bridge across the river from their settlement...they should have built the church on the side where they lived! If Dad had yet another baseball cap with an inscription that described his thinking, it would include his last name in the slogan, declaring, THE WRIGHT WAY. I can almost hear Frank Sinatra singing Dad's theme song...."My Way!" Dad was a man of few words, only half-heartedly embracing the concepts of compromise, negotiation or discussion. God gave Dad 94 years to teach his family what was "right," and yet, all I wanted was to hear him say, "I love you."

The last time I saw my Dad, I realized that I would never have that clarity as I held his hand during "social time" at the nursing home.

LOOKIN' FOR LOVE IN ALL THE WRONG PLACES

He slumped in his wheel chair in front of the busy nurses' station. My heart was anything but celebratory even though his wife, children and their spouses had shared his favorite angel food birthday cake a few days earlier in honor of Dad's amazing 94 year journey. The dementia-stressed lady sitting on the other side of his wheel chair ranted continuously about the screen door that wouldn't stop banging. My husband, sister and I listened patiently to what turned out to be final thoughts. Dad saluted his youngest daughter, "who had been so helpful in keeping his affairs straight; what would he have done without her??" He proclaimed that "Marjorie had done the right thing by calling frequently and coming home every year for Christmas," but he was still furious with his wife's mother (deceased more than 50 years) who wanted to put him in prison for getting her 15 year old daughter pregnant. Above all else, Dad took pride in the fact that his marriage had lasted 73 years, which, when it began in 1937, few gave much of a chance.

I left the nursing home aching for his overt approval . A few weeks after my last visit and return to our Minnesota home, he was gone. I had longed for that loving approval not only for myself, but for all of my siblings, and especially for my mother! She never complained. She loved my Dad unconditionally "for better or worse" for all 73 years of their marriage. Together, they "made it!"

I had hoped for a different ending to Dad's story, wanting a different feeling about our relationship. I wondered, had I misjudged, misunderstood, or misinterpreted my Dad's stiffness, tough exterior, bull-headedness? I went back to the beginning....

Dad's parents, John Urban Wright and Florence May Hale of Clinton, Indiana, were married on January 31st, 1911, and began their married life as farmers. Florence was one of 3 daughters raised by their father, while their mother spent the last years of her life in a sanitarium. A daughter, Opal Lucille, was born to John U and Florence a year after their marriage. A son, Ulysses Grant, arrived four years later on New Year's Eve, 1916.

Thirteen years later, during those neuron-exploding days of Dad's

FATHER, MAY I...

adolescence, the relentless blows of hardship and failure began to fall. The deck was stacked against Dad and the tables were unexpectedly turned at every corner during this vulnerable period in his young life. A chronology of Dad's devastating experiences is depicted below, indicating his age, the date and the event:

<u>Age</u>	<u>Date</u>	<u>Event</u>
13	1929	Beginning of the **Great Depression** (ended in the late 30's)
15	1931	**Bankruptcy:** Representatives of the bank and owners of the Horace Link furniture store came to the farm and threatened to take possession of the farm if the Wrights could not meet their financial obligations. It wasn't until after U.G.'s death at age 94 that my sister discovered, upon studying the abstract for the farm, that the Illinois Trust Company, holder of the farm's mortgage, actually failed during the Depression. The First National Bank and Trust took over the Illinois Trust Company and its holdings, including the Wright's mortgage. According to the abstract, the bank called in the loan to the Wrights for $11,240.80. When it became apparent that John U. and Florence did not have the money to pay the loan off or pay the Horace Link Furniture Store bill amounting to $328.40, the court declared John U. bankrupt on September 28, 1931. The sheriff was instructed by the court to serve John U. **foreclosure** papers on November 9, 1931. According to the abstract, the farm was sold at public auction to the Nelson Title Company.
18	1934	On July 14, 1934, the **farm land was resold** to John U. Wright for $9,000 when a loan from the Federal Land Bank of St. Louis for $6,000 was

approved. This loan was granted due to the support and advice of S. I. Headley, grandfather of Kathryn Gilbert who was 13 years old at the time. Steven Independence Headley, County Judge, was Chairman of the Agricultural Adjustment Board of Edgar County, enabling hundreds of farmers to negotiate loans which prevented them from losing their farms throughout and following the Great Depression.

Age	Year	Event
18	1935	Graduated from high school, U.G. was a good looking young man who excelled in math and basketball. Shortly after graduation, he made the decision to turn his back on a farming career and enroll in nearby Indiana State Teachers College to become a basketball coach. He hung up his overalls, donned a pair of dress slacks and prepared to drive 25 miles to a different world. Ulysses Grant Wright didn't make it out of the driveway, choosing instead the familiarity of home. Dad's confidence was rattled. Soon, the 19 year old was planting crops behind a team of horses, hauling grain and feeding hogs and cattle alongside his father.
19	1936	Attracted to Kathryn Jane Gilbert, PHS 10th grader; summer romance resulted in **pregnancy**
20	1937	April 24, 1st child, a boy, born in Kansas City and adopted the next month by undisclosed family currently residing in Kansas City
20	1937	July 7, Kathryn and U.G. "eloped" and were married in Terre Haute, IN
22	1939	Start of **WWII** in Europe
22	1939	Great Depression subsided
22	1939	April 15 – 2nd child, Martha Jane born
24	1941	July 9, **Martha Jane died** of Peritonitis, after swallowing broken glass from a drinking glass (age: 2 years, 2 months, 24 days)

FATHER, MAY I...

25	1942	February Howard Whalen (Pat) Gillespy and U.G.'s sister, Opal were married
25	1942	May 19 – 3rd child, John Henry born
25	1942	September 3, Father, John U. Wright, died
26	1943	August 31 – 4th child, Marjorie born
27	1944	"Pat" Gillespy (brother-in-law was killed in Italy, days away from military discharge)
28	1945	End of WWII in the Pacific
29	1946	March 18 – 5th child, Patricia born
30	1947	Lost coveted job as rural mail carrier when the young men returned home from the war
50	1966	August 6—Marjorie married and on the eve of her wedding, U.G. and Kathryn's first child called, identifying himself to his birth parents
50	1966	August 21—U.G., Kathryn, their youngest daughter, and U.G.'s mother travel to Oklahoma to meet their 29 year old son
In	1937	Dad had little choice but to grasp his harsh reality and take on a mantle of responsibility, staring at an unknown future that threw away his youth, exchanging it for fear and uncertainty. Meanwhile, sixteen-year-old Kathryn returned to her parents' home near Paris, recovering from the trauma of giving birth, the social stigma of "unwed mother" and the heart-wrenching grief of "giving up" her newborn son. Kathryn's mother forbid Kathryn and U.G. the right to be together, threatening to send U.G. to the penitentiary if he tried to see her daughter. When the young couple "ran away" to get married, Kathryn's parents refused to acknowledge their marriage and disowned Kathryn, their oldest daughter. Following the courthouse wedding in Terre Haute and with $6 in Dad's pocket, the young couple returned to U.G.'s parents' home and began married life near family, friends

and neighbors who whispered "the marriage will never last."

Living in the same house with Dad's parents in those first few years of marriage was challenging. Mom started married farm life knowing how to make lemonade and fudge. U.G.'s father continued to suffer with the bitter taste of bankruptcy and foreclosure. Stories of U.G.'s father reflected a strict taskmaster, who succumbed on occasion to the destructive results of alcohol. Life was no picnic, but the young couple persevered. The arrival of Kathryn and U.G.'s second baby was a beautiful blessing, a second chance to cherish a child of their own. U.G.'s father adored the little blond angel, who in her joyful infancy reconciled Kathryn and her parents. When Martha bit a drinking glass and swallowed tiny bits that ripped her insides, her death left guilt and grief in her parents' hearts for the rest of their lives. Fourteen months later, Dad's father died and at age 25, Dad was forced to "stuff" his feelings and engage in a "full court press" upon the family soil.

Day by day, corn row by corn row, jar after jar of canned vegetables, gallons of cream and cottage cheese, butchered hogs, baled hay, endless chores of gathering, weighing and sorting eggs, butchering chickens by wringing their heads off and plucking their boiling hot, stinky feathers, life was grueling, but predictable. A young adult male and his teen-age bride headed bravely into the future on a farm in Edgar County, continuing to strengthen their shared resolve to "make it."

Simultaneously, under the ever-darkening skies of a world gone awry....a world war compelled Uncle Sam's patriotic young men to drop everything and fight for America's freedom. Young farmers were deferred from active duty, and somewhat begrudgingly, were left behind to figure out how to survive in an economy that rationed food, clothing, and gas, along with the fun and spontaneity that had previously accompanied lives of predictability and safety. Crashing across those ominous clouds in daily living were lightning bolts of harsh reality....the chance for a second child, her birth and traumatic death, a repossessed farm, hail storms that ruined crops, and shadows of uncertainty that made little room for "sunshine."

U.G. never owned a credit card and he refused to give anyone his social security number. He was one of a handful of Americans who persuaded "the powers to be" to mail his Social Security check to his home as opposed to the millions of Americans who accepted the edict of "direct deposit." Dad firmly stated that "no one would deposit his check in the bank but himself!" He won the argument and insisted that "you got to look 'em in the eye," whether he was buying a bolt for the tractor or completing a transaction at the bank. He fiercely protected what was his, he abhorred being in debt and banks were "risky business."

Dad treasured a Letter of Commendation from the Farm Bureau touting his farming achievement of 200 bushels of corn to the acre. With help from his mother, he proudly put his three children through college and a son through dental school. The day my brother hung out the shingle opening his new dental office was a day of unprecedented pride and joy!

Throughout much of his life, and analogous to his love for basketball, "fouls" often interfered with Dad's determination to "make it." He never quit trying to make "a go" of life, continuing to toss the ball in the air, aiming for the hoop of success. With quiet, yet extraordinary effort, Kathryn and U.G. managed and eventually owned a successful, debt-free farm, one of the first color TV's in the neighborhood, a new car every three years, three children who graduated from college debt-free, an air-conditioned tractor, a son who played basketball and opened a dental office in the home town, daughters who became teachers and a marriage that lasted for 73 years. He believed that his legacy rested firmly in the children and grandchildren who cherished each other and were part of the "Wright" family, regardless of their last names.

God implores us to pay attention so that we might have understanding. He tells us that gaining wisdom is the most important thing

LOOKIN' FOR LOVE IN ALL THE WRONG PLACES

we can do. Whatever else we get, aim for insight! If I have any regrets about my Dad, it is how slowly I accumulated that awareness. Most of my life, I wished for a more demonstrative dad who would use his words and warm hugs to say "I love you." Had I paid closer attention, I would have seen and understood the wisdom and love that was there all along.

Someone who loved me helped me get ready to show off animal projects during 4-H Tours. Someone who loved me trusted me to do my chores without reminders (gather the eggs; care for 4-H pigs, baby turkeys, chickens, sheep and Angus or Hereford cattle, help with meal preparation and the dishes, take care of garden duties, pull weeds in acres and acres of soybeans). Someone who loved me chased and caught the horse that took off with a scared little girl hanging for dear life onto the horse's mane. Someone who loved me made sure that we tasted home-grown strawberries, home-grown beef, home-grown chicken and eggs (all organic....long before we knew what that meant) and homemade ice cream. Someone who loved me built crackling fires in the living room and wrapped hot bricks into blankets to keep our feet warm on cold winter nights. Someone who loved me tried to teach me how to milk a cow and laughed when that "dang" cow stepped on my foot and remained there in spite of the intense hammering of a ten-year-old's fists! Someone who loved me made sure every Christmas was magical, even when there wasn't much under the tree. Someone who loved me made sure I had a quiet place to study, a college education and ultimately squelched his "rather be home" desires to drive 750 miles to watch his daughter don the mantle of "doctor" at the University of Minnesota.

Someone who loved me did not make me feel guilty for heading to a new life in Minnesota as a newlywed and wholeheartedly accepted my husband as one of the family. Someone who loved me remembered and valued my help with chores in our home and on the farm. He was proud of my achievements in school. Like the country song, I was "looking for love in all the wrong places." Today, I find great joy in reflecting on Dad's wisdom, understanding his fierce determination and feeling so grateful for all that he sacrificed to ensure a safe, healthy and meaningful life for the children he loved.

When I sat with Dad during our last time together, he spoke vehemently about his mother-in-law wanting to send him to prison. He expressed his gratitude for my frequent phone calls and commitment to coming home every Christmas to spend time with the family. Clouds and storms often loomed large in the backdrop of his life, but in spite of the hardships and the stressors that nailed Dad early in his life, I felt his satisfaction for a life authentically lived. I know that in his tired smile, he was wanting to shout to many, "I told you so!"

Today, I am grateful that the feelings that often dictate how we experience life, can change because we <u>choose</u> to think about and see things differently. Walaa! Our feelings can turn a corner or reverse completely! Much of Dad's strength, determination and value for family rubbed off on his children. When the final buzzer sounded, ending Dad's game on this earthly court, and he headed off to a heavenly venue, a tender feeling began to grow in my heart. My small hand remembered holding the short, thick, stubby, calloused fingers of a loving Dad. I knew that my heart had found what I was looking for.

Heroes In a Box

WHEN I WAS growing up, kids had lots of heroes like Roy Rogers, Lone Ranger, Cisco Kid, Sky King....some even classified as Super Heroes...Superman and Batman. These heroes came alive in comic book pages or in the TV box. Howdy Doody and Buster Brown lived there too. I don't think I spent much time revering these "guys" as heroes...maybe because they were all male and dressed differently.

My favorite childhood "TV Box" heroes were cute and talented. Annette Funicello (my favorite Mouseketeer) and Janet Lennon (who is still performing with female vocalists as a "Lennon sister" from the Lawrence Welk show) were my all-time favorites. My heroes came alive in books as they solved mysteries (Nancy Drew), helped heal people (Sue Barton, Nurse), or overcame tremendous life challenges in stories like The Secret Garden or Little Women.

Superman and Batman were still popular when our children arrived at the hero stage. Our son added Incredible Hulk and Evil Kneivel heroes and the girls relished Wonder Woman and Barbie as "favorites," setting the stage for hours and hours of play. Sesame Street offered a different kind of superstars, the likes of Big Bird, the Count and even Oscar, who focused on developing character instead of fighting crime. My favorite Superhero story finds our three children standing behind me near the outdoor ticket booth at the St. Cloud Paramount Movie Theater on a Saturday afternoon. The kids were super-excited to see Superman on the big screen. The ticket clerk announced, "that will be $5.00 and we do not accept checks." I grimaced as I realized that I had not brought any cash. Andrea (age 5) says in her quiet little voice as she quickly snaps open her tiny little pink purse, "I have money!" Our Super Kid saved the day with a tightly folded $5 bill!

Other daytime "TV Box" favorites included Captain Kangaroo and Mr. Rogers. Our children even enjoyed a Christmas breakfast with Captain Kangaroo in our home town. A few years ago, an article on the internet spoke of Captain Kangaroo and Fred Rogers as war heroes prior to coming home to America to dedicate their lives leading children down the right path. Bob Keeshan was reportedly admired as a marine sergeant at the initial landing at Iwo Jima in World War II. The story described Keeshan standing up on more than one occasion, as the main target of gunfire at Iwo Jima so that his men could get to safety. Most of us only knew the man who donned a red jacket and assumed the gentle character of Captain Kangaroo, aiming for our children and others to know the safety and love of caring adults.

Quiet, gentle Mr. Rogers was acclaimed as well on the Internet, as a U.S. Navy Seal in Vietnam. Fred Rogers was said to have covered the many tattoos on his forearm and biceps with his long-sleeved sweaters. Our children spent lots of time in Mister Rogers' neighborhood subconsciously absorbing his message of "you are special." Both Keeshan and Rogers were praised for rededicating their lives to teaching the values and morals of American families and fostering freedom by choosing a path of kindness and self-respect.

I later learned an important lesson about investigation and truth. There was no truth in the stated war achievements of either Captain Kangaroo or Mister Rogers. In spite of the claim of actor Lee Marvin, Bob Keeshan did not fight in the battle for Iwo Jima, nor did he take part in any World War II action. Folklorists, who study how people express themselves in everyday life, say that the stories we tell about public figures, like Captain Kangaroo can actually tell us a lot about ourselves. Do we want to be what we invent about others?

While initially working in television in Pittsburg, Mr. Rogers felt a call to pursue seminary studies, and expressed his ministry in a PBS children's television show, as a deft puppeteer and storyteller. Rogers had a deep love of—and respect for—children, filling 33 years of programming with gentle lessons and simple entertainment.

Heroes play a critical role in the lives of not only children, but adults. Without heroes, we lose our desire to seek and emulate others who demonstrate courage, selflessness, humility, patience and caring. Heroes are becoming increasingly scarce in our American culture of violence, political divisiveness, selfishness and instant gratification. Our world so desperately needs superheroes today. It is imperative that we release our superwomen and supermen, who are increasingly trapped in boxes of FEAR! In today's world, it's going to take nearly all of us to "save the day!"

Keep a Song in Your Heart

THE MEANING OF the word "trifecta" originated as a bet in which the person betting forecasts the first three finishers in any race in the correct order. Interpretation of the word has expanded to mean "outstanding triple achievement" in show business, sports or even a winning meal of appetizers, main course and dessert. A trifecta can be "dark" too and most would agree that the days between March 2020 and December 2021 spiraled into a Covid 19 trifecta of fear, drastic lifestyle change and loneliness. The world is clamoring to move on to a life worth living....an urgent need to generate faith in a new, positive trifecta! Who isn't challenged trying to squeeze calmness, civility, social reengagement, safety, hope and gratitude back into the toolbox of daily life? It is crucial that we return to the old definition of positivity that lights our eyes and smiles with joy, kindness and meaning. To jumpstart a Post-Covid Trifecta, I consider a triple-G "trifecta" of persons who are well-grounded in "gumption, grit and goodwill!" Perhaps you have heard of them.... (1) Deborah Birx; (2) Stephen Wamukot and (3) Lawrence Welk.

The past 700 days, like no other, have challenged our well-being and faith, hinting that there may never be the kind of "normal" again like we have known. I remain gratefully reassured by heroes who unselfishly care for the sick, develop a cure or establish strategies to keep us protected in the meantime. One 3-G person, with worldly dreams, bigger than the entire universe of science and medicine, is Deborah Birx. Dr. Birx, a physician, former US Army colonel and global health expert, is renowned for extraordinary HIV/AIDS research in the US. During the unexpected worldwide explosion of Covid-19, Birx was appointed by former United States VP Mike Pence as the response coordinator for the coronavirus task force. Dr. Birx became Pence's right arm in navigating the covid crisis. Dr. Birx became Pence's right arm in navigating the covid crisis. Dr. Birx unrelentingly strived to focus attention and resolution on the huge disconnect between clinical data systems, what happens at laboratories and hospitals and our public health data systems.

Many will remember Dr. Birx (during 2020 White House news briefings) for the beautiful scarves that she wore so gracefully (her own smart traveling strategy....one dress, many scarves). Of far greater significance is her life's work in worldwide data research and systems connections in partnership with genome researchers and epidemiologists... foundational work that will define the future of our world's health. Dr. Birx shared her agonizing covid coordinator journey during a January 24, 2021 interview with Lesley Stahl on CBS's Sixty Minutes. Gumption, grit and goodwill kept Dr. Brix's 3-G force powerful in the face of critics and knuckleheads, who often squelched or overlooked the value of her 24-7 efforts on behalf of all human beings. Dr. Birx "never, never, never, ever wanted to jump into a White House, highly politicized role." Yet, courage and brilliance drove Dr. Birx's quest for life-saving data corroboration, relative to the covid pandemic, in partnership with millions of scientific and medical experts all over the globe. How can we not celebrate the brilliant mind of Deborah Birx and the caring heart that beat with determined purpose beneath those beautiful scarves?

The Red Tricycle, an organization whose mission was to connect families and create memories, shared stories across the world about children like Stephen Wamukota. Stephen, a young boy in Mukwa, Kenya, represents my second trifecta nominee for "outstanding achievement" in an attempt to define life worth living. Stephen, nine years old, designed a hand-wash station that tipped water from a bucket with the use of a pedal that avoids touching surfaces, reducing infection. So many children like Stephen wanted to help fight Covid. Other budding entrepreneurs, Brianna and Ashley Wong, 9 and 6 year old sisters, made keychains and bracelets, donating their profits to international organizations.

Seventeen year old Avi, created a website with information on global and local Covid stats, a preparation site, a Q and A section and a map showing the outbreaks of the virus. Her purpose was to correct misinformation. When she reached out to news agencies, none responded until much later, after Avi's site attracted thousands of viewers.

In Tennessee, as the Covid Pandemic got underway, 11 year old Lucy made over 1100 masks in a couple of months to distribute to health workers. Ten year old Sydney and her Mom wrote, recorded and animated four You tube videos entitled "Kids Coping with Covid 19." Twelve-year-old Dominic asked for boxes of pasta and jars of spaghetti sauce for the food shelf instead of a birthday party. The donations were enough to fill 5 SUV's and over 100 people drove to Dominic's to pick up and deliver the goods. Chelsea still collects art supplies instead of presents at birthday parties to give to kids in homeless shelters and foster homes.

Children did, and continue to do <u>big</u> things. Teen-agers, Alex and Ben, started an online tutoring service for kids. Kind children, empathetic for others, also did <u>little</u> things. Curtis created a prom for his babysitter, when her high school prom was covid-canceled. Nine year old Curtis dressed in a suit and bowtie and escorted his high school babysitter, Rachell, to a Chick-Filet dinner in his back yard. Rachell wore a long gown and dancing followed, with a swimming pool noodle between them to ensure dancing six feel apart.

There are thousands of stories like these that speak of the kindness and unselfish efforts of children, families and other adults. So many demonstrated amazing innovation and goodwill through their unselfish efforts to help sick, poor, hungry, fearful and struggling human beings who had been frightened into a downward spiral. Those who gave time, talent and treasure were rewarded simply, and sincerely, with gratitude.

Even those who were "managing" Covid 19 successfully, were inspired by the "end-of-news-show" stories that lifted sagging spirits, rekindling faith in our shared humanity. During those short glimpses, it was easier to believe "we were going to make it."

A third nomination for a trifecta of "life worth living" is Lawrence Welk, to whom many of us were introduced a long time ago. With every "anna 1, anna 2," Lawrence delighted audiences young and old with his infectious smile, joyful dancing, songs to swing and sway to and easy-listening orchestrations of music that made his audiences feel happy. It has been definitely challenging to find "happy" in these days of covid stress, further muddied by endless political squawking and finger-pointing.

In 1958, Saturday nights in my home were joyfully anticipated on our brand-new Zenith TV. The 12 inch screen had one channel and an on-off button that you actually had to get out of the chair to operate. Right in our living room, we were enthralled with cowboy shows, hilarious comedies, Walter Cronkite...even the "test pattern" and the upbeat Lawrence Welk Show.

The iridescent champagne bubbles had begun "popping" LIVE on station KTLA Los Angeles in 1951, the first commercial television station airing west of the Mississippi River, bordering my home state of Illinois. Through unimaginable magic, I watched Lawrence, the Lennon Sisters (DeeDee, Peggy, Cathy and Janet), dancers Bobby and Barbara, Elaine or Cissy, Myron Floren, Larry Hooper, Arthur Duncan, Joe Feeney, Norma Zimmer, Ava Barber, Mary Lou Metzger, JoAnn Castle and all of Lawrence's Musical Family, as it continued to grow. Even the show's sponsors delivered happy—"gonna' make you feel good" messages..... a life-enhancing Dodge, Geritol for tired blood, Aqua Velva (awake and away with the face that's fit), Sominex (when you can't sleep), Serutan (gets you regular), Polident (keeps your dentures white and bright). And....the best motivation of all...being together with the whole family in our living room.

Like the doctors, nurses, paramedics, law enforcement personnel and everyday citizens who continue to risk their own lives for the physical well-being of others, Lawrence's charm and talent sought to emotionally "lift" his audience of millions. Welk's 3-G force, expressed through the music of "big band," talented singers and energetic dancers, was unleashed in 1951, 70 years ago. In spite of Lawrence's retirement at age 79 and death ten years later in 1992, Champagne Music lives on. I am grateful for Public Broadcasting Stations who continue to connect Americans with Lawrence's bubbles and his Musical Family of musicians, singers, composers, dancers and costume designers.

Lawrence Welk Album

Lawrence Welk's "polka to success" required Gumption, Grit, and Goodwill. Welk represents millions of photographers, chefs, sculptors, painters, quilters, playwrights, performers and entrepreneurs. Artists' gifts have the power to strengthen and heal our souls through unique, creative beauty that dazzles our senses through sight, sound, touch, smell and taste.

KEEP A SONG IN YOUR HEART

We will struggle to find our way back to happy, safe, kind, interactive and productive lives in the days, months and years post-Covid 19, but we will "pick ourselves up, dust ourselves off" and start anew creating "outstanding achievement" in every facet of science, humanity and beauty. There is no first, second, third place winner in a post-Covid Trifecta. We are all winners when we pursue the one, true Trifecta, always ready to guide our journey..... our Father, His Son and the Holy Spirit, a trifecta of Faith. God will always nurture the resiliency of the human mind and spirit, encouraging our talents in creating a life worth living. Perhaps, Lawrence was preparing us for post-Covid life over these past 60 years as he passed along God's optimistic advice at the end of each show.... "keep a song in your heart."

No Scars

I HAVE A one inch scar on my right wrist that is the result of an overzealous 10 year old's sprint through the house. My Aunt Opal, who lived in El Paso, Texas was soon to arrive for a visit with her brother (my Dad) and his family. The tree lights were twinkling, the stockings were hung and the smells of a turkey dinner set the stage for company on our farm in central Illinois and it was Christmas. When the crunch on the crushed rock driveway signaled Aunt Opal's arrival, I leaped out of my chair and raced for the back porch where I knew she would enter with a huge smile and outstretched arms, ready for long-overdue hugs!

Sixty-eight years ago, I raced through the kitchen, onto the back porch and shoved open the glass storm door with surprising strength for a ten year old. My arm smashed through the glass with a bloody mess and screams greeting our long-awaited visitor! The wound was massive, messy and mortifying. Bandaged quickly and neatly by Mom, the wound healed over the next few weeks and only the scar remains of my mad dash. I don't remember the pain. I can't really visualize the mess and I certainly don't carry any emotional scars from that painful accident...... but I do glance at the scar on my arm every once in awhile, remembering Aunt Opal......and the memory is good.

I do wonder about scars likely to remain long after the Covid-19 Pandemic is behind us. Most of the scars will not be visible, but devastating deaths in the millions, economic ramifications and unprecedented halts on social interaction are bound to take a mental toll, leaving so many scars we cannot see. The Center for Disease Control reports 10% of adults in the US showed symptoms of depression during the 9 months between July 2019 – March 2020. Three months later, that percentage had doubled. Studies and surveys conducted so far during the pandemic indicate that young people, rather than older people, are most vulnerable to increased psychological distress, perhaps because their needs for social interactions are stronger. So what can I do to protect myself from those invisible scars?

> Make myself a No-Scar Checklist to keep my spirts high, focusing on wellness!
> I started with C......
> C Covid 19 Vaccine: Two doses plus booster Check!
> O Opportunities: Smile, greet and engage with strangers
> N News on TV....Turn on less of it
> N Notice the world: And express gratitude for beautiful things each day
> E Exercise: in the morning with a walk or fitness video
> C Call: friends, family and those who have experienced loss
> T Text: jokes, pictures, quotes or scripture to children and grandchildren

My goal is to ramp up my personal positivity efforts. My own PPE. My strategy spells CONNECT. A projected analysis of my Connect Checklist predicts….. "No Scars!"

Rescued

HE LAY SILENTLY on the floor, too weak to bark or lift his head, Meeting the intensity of their gazes with sad, blue eyes....pleading "will you rescue me?"

Abandoned in a back yard, trapped in the blazing sun's heat, body hair burning,

Deserted with a pool of water and bag of food,

Loneliness oozed from his electric blue eyes, pleading... someone, anyone...

"Will you rescue me?"

Carried to shelter safety, broken in spirit, diminished body strength,

Greeting each visitor with piercing blue eyes silently messaging... will you rescue me?

Skeleton protruding under emaciated hide,

Loving blue eyes continuing to beg....will you rescue me?

Survivor of neglect, looking anything but "adorable,"

Our eyes met hopeful blue ones clearly imploring, "will you rescue me?"

"No".... an option, but quickly discarded;

Suffering, reflected in liquid orbs of blue, weighed on caring hearts;

No indecision. A new member was adopted into the family.

Easton became his new name, mistaking his origin as Chesapeake Bay Retriever.

Food was savored and appreciated; it must arrive promptly at 5.

Daylight Savings Time was hard to handle;
Return to Central Standard was just as discombobulating.
Car rides were his happy place, and walks were delightfully shared.
Loving was Easton's best talent; those eyes just locked each human gaze.
Easton engaged, appreciating each treat, lengthy ear scratch, or vigorous tummy rub,
Rewarding with a snuggle close by.
Delivering companionship, offering comfort and celebrating with family for eleven busy years kept Easton happily attentive.
Expressing sorrow only when commitments took his family elsewhere;
Easton happily greeting with intense blue eyes and tail-wagging joy upon their return.
As pain began to creep into Easton's aging bones and muscles,
He barked an intense cry of discomfort when shifting, standing or sitting.
Suffering blue eyes once again implored, "will you rescue me?"
Anguish filled the hearts of Easton's "besties."
Indecision clouded dwindling days as Easton's suffering grew worse.
Thoughts of good-bye lay heavy.
God intervened; Heaven painted a joyful picture of "running pain free and eating anything and everything that [Easton's] heart desired,
No longer could there be denial of his final earthly request, "will you rescue me?"
As the days drifted by, remembering the gift and spirit of Easton uplifted.
Recognition of gratitude for Easton's presence through years of ups and downs
filled memories,
Smiles are sad, remembering loving hugs and scratches,
So joyfully received by this lumbering, soft blue-eyed angel.

FATHER, MAY I...

Easton was cherished, he softened life's blows;
He brought smiles and laughter, and never stopped lighting lives with love.
Your family is grateful, Easton. Perhaps it was you, who "rescued" them.

Ain't No Mountain High Enough

Chicken Little's Warning

MANY SATURDAY EVENINGS in the spring, summer and fall of the early 1950's, Mom and Dad drove my brother, sister and I seven miles into our small town in Illinois as a special treat. The evening started with sitting on the low cement wall surrounding the imposing County Courthouse. Our parents visited with friends on those warm, summer evenings, while the kids jumped on and off of the wall and chased each other until parents decided it was time to go. If we hadn't been too ornery, the family stopped at Elam's Ice Cream Store for a vanilla cone. That prize was followed by one more short, but essential detour before we returned to the farm.

Driving down a near-by side street brought us to a long, cracked sidewalk across the street from a local business called Frye's Hatchery. In large painted letters on the side of the brick building, the long-time business proclaimed, "We Raise Frye's Chicks." As three pairs of eyes peered through the 1950 Chevrolet's back window, looking up at the huge yellow NEON sign attached to the building, we chirped in between licks of ice cream, "egg....crack...chicken!" Our game was to perfectly time shouts of "egg, crack, chicken" with the sign's three distinct changes. The sign proclaimed Frye's Hatchery as a chick business—nurturing eggs that would hatch into baby chicks. The "twilight zone" sign was pure magic as it changed from an.....egg......to a crack.....and finally a fuzzy little chicken popping out of the cracked shell. I have no idea how many times we sat and recited those three little words, but 60+ years later, I am convinced that I would only

FATHER, MAY I...

need to utter the word "egg" to my siblings …… and "crack" … "chicken" would follow.

If the word "simplicity" characterized a "night out on the square" in my home town, I wonder what word would capture the essence of entertainment for a family evening 70 years later? I grew up on a farm with two hard-working parents, a bucketload of chores, a brother, a sister and a couple of family secrets, revealed after my childhood had been safely, morally and happily completed. Today, as I weigh the impact of disappearing boundaries culturally, politically and socially, along with the challenges of poverty, homelessness, civil rights, discrimination, gender inequality, health care, political stagnation and obesity, I am reminded of the "crack in the egg" at Frye's Hatchery. I see in America an increasingly downward spiraling "brokenness." Old-fashioned values and morality are "cracking" at a scary pace as the protective shells of families, neighborhoods and moral leadership at all levels become increasingly fragile.

In a world where Americans seem to be chasing everything, we race to crack open new ideas and solutions for old problems. We break vehicles and bones when technology distracts our attention. We botch mindfulness, relationships and spirituality, zooming through work, family life and pursuit of happiness. It's all about "Selfie!" Even when immediate or end-goals are reached, the results are probably not what they were originally cracked up to be. Clothing advertisers proudly suggest how to cover cracks. Claiming pursuit of modesty and good taste, a company's ingenious, little bit of extra fabric on the Longtail Shirt, solved an age-old problem: the embarrassing, exposed Plumber's Crack!

"Crack" also presents itself in compound words. A crackpot is an eccentric or foolish person. A wisecrack is a glib, facetious or sardonic remark. Endings change "crack" to "cracker," referencing saltines or a thousand other kinds of crispy, crumbly wafers. "Cracker" is also offensive slang, a derogatory term for a white person, primarily heard in the US. A positive use of cracker is found in the word "crackerjack," a tasty treat, or a person regarded as outstanding or superb in some endeavor. As a verb, when we "crack up" at hilarious cartoons or spoofy jokes, we burst into laughter. Yet, when suffering an emotional breakdown under pressure, we might lament, while on the verge of tears, "I'm cracking up!"

Increasingly, crack has come to mean something sinister and ugly. Crack cocaine, also known simply as crack or rock, is a form of cocaine that can be smoked. Crack offers a short, intense high to smokers. The Manual of Adolescent Substance Abuse Treatment calls it the most addictive form of cocaine. Crack's rapid, widespread use and availability is sometimes termed the "crack epidemic." The resulting brokenness around this epidemic is the antithesis of the fuzzy, yellow chick that emerged from the crack in the neon sign at Frye's Hatchery.

If I had the pleasure of sitting across the street from Frye's Hatchery today, I would search for a positive response to negative declarations... ."crack in the egg," " break in the armor," "fly in the ointment," "hell breaking loose," "return to square one," "beating around the bush," "barking up the wrong tree," "chips on shoulders," "hitting below the belt," or "throwing in the towel." I visualize the sweet, tiny yellow chick emerging from "brokenness," as a messenger, peeping instead, loving requests to "knock it out of the park," "swing for the fence," "roll with the punches," "note the absence of I in TEAM," "slop happy as a pig in mud," "float on cloud nine" or "walk in sunshine."

At Frye's Hatchery, a thriving business more than half a century ago in Paris, Illinois, the peeps of thousands of newborn baby chicks created a melodic, distinctive song of unity. That chorus of tiny peeps emerging from stacks of cardboard crates, brought smiles of peace and gentleness to all who walked nearby. The newly hatched chicks' instinctive snuggling together, protecting one another from the cold, early Spring, parallels the safety and comfort craved by nearly all human beings in our divisive world.

Our 21st Century sky feels like it is falling. We are all "Chicken Littles" in the scheme of neighborhood and global survival. Amanda Gorman, poet laureate at President Biden's 2021 Inauguration, spoke of a "nation that isn't broken, but simply unfinished." Can we accept

FATHER, MAY I...

the challenge that "finishing" is inherent upon each one of us?

I speak for myself, ready to peck my way through shells of reluctance. I seek God's encouragement to hop off my comfortable "roost," as my household and community awaken each day. I resolve to strut confidently forward, ready to dig deeper within opportunities to grow stronger in voice, kindness and intentional action. Lifting the well-being of humankind, one human at a time is my goal. My personal commitment can no longer hide behind fearful concerns that "the sky is falling!" Today is the day for action and it's time to get 'crackin!'

Sometimes You Win, Sometimes You Learn

DAD LOVED BASKETBALL his entire life and upon high school graduation, enrolled at Indiana State College, aspiring to become a basketball coach. According to the story passed down, prior to the first class, he hung up his new pants, put his bib overalls back on and said "that's not for me!"

In a brilliant burst of insight, nearly 50 years later, my sister signed Dad up as a volunteer coach at the local YMCA for 5th and 6th grade boys and girls. To ensure his commitment for the long haul, my sister stepped to Dad's side as Assistant Coach.

Throughout his lifetime of loving the game of basketball, Dad's mantra was "free throws win ballgames!" His baseball cap displayed that message and he never let his young players forget it. Dad insisted that his elementary-age ball players practice 100 free throws each day and his "no goofin' around" strategy worked as he transformed chatty girls and boys full of horseplay, into "personal best" champions year after year.

Role modeling for his "players" even got him out of his bib overalls and resulted in life-changing testimonials from many young boys and girls. He loved being Coach, and his players loved him. One of my favorite stories is of a very tall 6th grader, who was falling behind in his school work and was soon to be pulled from the YMCA basketball team by his mother. Dad talked to six-footer's mother....asked

FATHER, MAY I...

for an extension....talked to the errant student....and told him that he needed to focus on his school work or he wouldn't be allowed to play basketball. Dad continued.... "just picture yourself bouncing that basketball down the floor in high school with all the girls screaming your name." A young man took his coach's advice and pulled off honor roll distinction the next quarter!

Dad was undeniably proud of his "Pool Team." During the annual team member selection process by the Y coaches, there was always a group of players last to be chosen, the "reject players" that no other coach wanted. Dad waited with his team "picks," and selected the remaining players as his "pool team." He took all of the "rejects," and worked hard to prepare them for their first game. With players in position and crowds cheering in the bleachers, one of the Pool Team starters zipped down the gym floor, unattended, and aimed for the net. The young "pool" player scored his first basket ever! The smile on his face lit up the gym. What a celebration, regardless of the fact that he scored a two-pointer for the opposing team!

Starting with the Pool Team, Dad bought socks for his players...."my athletes should not be embarrassed by socks with holes." Every player was recognized at the year end banquet for an accomplishment (most free throws, best attitude, most improved or simply showed up for practice). Players worked hard for Dad. He expected nothing less and he molded "champions," with a can of coke after each game, an award for each player at the end of each season and a belief in each of them. At the annual award ceremony in a local restaurant (funded by Mom and Dad), each player was MVP and got a tiny trophy for skill or effort. He also rewarded the small town boys and girls with much anticipated trips to a nearby city to enjoy the world famous Globe Trotters.

Dad's commitment to basketball eventually included all of his hometown grandchildren! I got to witness a handful of those games and marveled at the "fathering" and "advising" he liberally showered upon his players. The grandchildren occasionally went "out of bounds" with Grampa. As coach, Dad tried out new "throw the other

SOMETIMES YOU WIN, SOMETIMES YOU LEARN

team off base" maneuvers. The players got in a huddle and started dancing in a circle. At the signaled moment, they were to burst out of the circle and attempt to confuse the other team by dancing to their positions. However, on the way out of the huddle, one of Coach U.G.'s grandsons said under his breath, "let's do it the way we always do it!"

One of Dad's girls' teams became the Illinois Junior High School State Champs. Dad followed his players through their high school careers and attended every home game each of them played. The accolades for Dad would not have been possible without a top notch assistant coach, a VCD (very committed daughter) at his side.

And Dad had Mom…ALWAYS his right hand at hundreds of games, keeping the "stats," handling communication details and encouraging "Coach" to continue a commitment to kids in their community. Mom cheered for the players, visited with their parents, bought the socks and kept the books while silently encouraging Dad to "live his dream." Whether on the court, in the field, at the kitchen table or near his bedside, Mom was a Life Coach. "So glad to see you today, Ronny. How are the free throws coming along? Hey, Sally, you had a great practice today. Keep up the good work. Johnny, how is your dad doing? If you need a ride to practice next week, let me know! Susie, look at the score book. You made 8 points today. Your parents were jumping off the bleachers!" and on and on. Mom wanted the young players to feel valued, essential contributors to a team effort and to enjoy positive recognition. Always, always, always…. players on the Pool Team felt, "I am valued!"

Thirty years after his retirement from coaching, many of Dad's YMCA "stars" came to the funeral home to share "lessons learned," to whisper "thanks," and "shoot" a grateful good-bye to the man who believed in them "on" and "off" the court. Standing beside the casket, Dad's Assistant Coach and his Right Hand Statistician tried to hold back tears of pride. A devoted wife and daughter had successfully ensured a young man's dream come true, supporting Coach Wright's philosophy that learning the lessons of life were game winners every time.

More to the Story

ON THE NIGHT of September 26, 2013, New York Yankee pitcher, Mariano Rivera was escorted off the field for the last time. With two outs in the ninth, teammates Andy Pettitte and Derek Jeter escorted Rivera out of a game that had lasted 19 seasons, with a record 652 saves. Rivera's last season became a farewell tour and Bronx tears were flowing as the man, who many call baseball's greatest relief pitcher, said goodbye.

Rivera's story will resonate for a long time among baseball fans and those who are not, as he transcended not only the sport but his rivals. With opposing fans applauding him throughout the final season, Rivera said, "I always treat the game the way you should treat it. I always treat the opposite team the way they should be treated. I always give respect. And you know, I think people appreciate what you do." Rivera pitched a great deal more than baseballs. I hope young and old heard the rest of Rivera's story.

A day or two later, in the small Minnesota town of Zimmerman, high school Homecoming Candidates surrendered the title of "King" during a pep fest to someone in the audience they felt was more deserving of the honor. When the time came to announce the 2013 Homecoming King, the four candidates leaped off the stage and carried the crown to place it on the head of a very surprised Jonah, who had struggled with the loss of a leg to cancer. The football team also named Jonah as an honorary member ....and students sold hot dogs during homecoming week to help the family with medical expenses.

Reporters describe the goosebump-raising cheers that filled the gymnasium and the tearful joy that filled the hearts of a school with a story that went so much deeper.

And in the same week, a story from Oklahoma City, where seventy-eight-year-old Tona Herndon was on her way to the car after burying her husband of 60 years. Her eyes were so clouded with grief, she never saw it coming. She was mugged and the mugger got away with her purse and $700. Police caught him, and the news put his mug shot on TV. The mugger's son, Christian, saw the picture and had no doubt that it was his dad. Christian says his parents divorced when he was two, and his dad has been mostly absent ever since. Last time he heard from him had been a few weeks ago. His dad gave him $250 for a band trip in which Christian really wanted to participate. Christian says that monetary gift had pretty much been the extent of his dad's parenting recently. In fact, over the years, Christian says his dad has been in and out of jail more than half a dozen times. "There's times that you just feel really low, like, 'Is that going to be me, he says. "Am I going to end up like that?" **I don't think so**.... Christian arranged to meet Tona and handed over the $250 with a heartfelt apology and expressed a strong desire not to end up following in his father's footsteps. Tona accepted the money and then gifted Christian with the money toward his long anticipated band trip. An amazing story of an amazing Christian!

And lastly, an unforgettable personal memory of stepping across the line to understand "more of the story."

During the eighties, my career path was focused in the area of community education. I had begun my teaching career at North Junior High in 1966, teaching girls about Home Economics (now branded as CFS or Consumer Family Science) and departed when the first little Hawkins came along. In the eighties, junior high students were moved to the high school building and Community Education enjoyed the luxury of occupying a building opened in 1965 for 1,200 7-9th grade students. Hoping to attract young learners, I wanted to replicate a national preschool program called *Safety Town*. It involved

FATHER, MAY I...

creating a pint-sized city with child-sized buildings that included a school, grocery store, bakery, gas station and a church. We planned to locate the "town" in the school's former Industrial Arts classroom. Special tape would mark the roads around the small buildings and we were eager to get the children on tricycles to follow the right side of the roads and practice "stoplight" rules as they "drove" around *Safety Town*. Some wonderful volunteers offered to make real stoplights that were six feet high and timed to flash green, yellow and red.

I was stuck on locating someone to make the 5' X 6' miniature buildings that would accommodate preschool play within the walls. A colleague suggested that I connect with "community service" volunteers. Without really understanding that "community service" options were sometimes available to law-breaking citizens who needed to work off part of a judge-decreed sentence, I arranged an interview with Mike K and his supervisor. Mike arrived at the school, his supervisor in tow, wearing dirty, threadbare jeans, a ripped shirt, unshaven and smelly. He was recommended by his community service officer as someone who knew his way around construction....he had access to a friend's barn and tools to construct the Safety Town buildings. Mike was eager to get his community service behind him, doing what he thought would be a lot more fun than picking up litter or cleaning up the city dump.

I stepped outside my comfort zone and said "ooooookayyyyyyy," and we set about creating blueprints on posterboard. Over several months, Mike kept in touch with a couple of phone calls and finally invited me out for a look. I kind of felt like I knew him by then and without any measure of common sense, hopped in our 1969 Plymouth and headed 5 miles out of town to the Barn. Mike was waiting for me in the doorway of the barn and when I realized it was just the two of us way out in the country in a secluded old barn, my heart was racing! Mike was so anxious to show me the work he had completed and I grabbed the first loose board...just in case!

Mike was muscular, strong...and his work was beautiful. The *Safety Town* buildings were finished, complete with window openings and doorways. He had painted them in bright primary colors with the building names painted on each structure. The only building without a name was the church, accented with steeple and cross. Mike and his supervisor arranged to have them delivered to the *Safety Town* Room at North Community Center. He hitched a ride with an acquaintance to North to help us lay out Safety Town, create the roads and parking areas and set up the red stop signs, which Mike had made as a surprise addition to our little town.

He worked at getting the lay-out "just right" for two days, appearing on the "outside" pretty much like the first day we had met. But, there was something different in the way he walked and organized the new little "town." And I couldn't help but notice the smile tugging at the corners of his mouth and a different light in his sad eyes. When I explained that we would celebrate the unveiling of *Safety Town* with a ribbon cutting ceremony, I told Mike that he really needed to be present to share in celebrating his accomplishment. I enthusiastically invited him to say a few words on that day. I let him know how much I appreciated all that he had done to create such a wonderful little town to teach safety to young children. Mike politely declined and said, "I don't think I could do that."

I left the door open, gave him the date and time and said, "I am **so proud** of what you have done....I really hope you will come and you don't have to say anything if you don't want to." The ribbon-cutting day arrived and at the last minute, around the corner came a jubilant Mike, wearing a slightly rumpled borrowed suit, a bright tie and the biggest smile on a clean-shaven face I had ever seen. When I introduced Mike as the "master-builder" who created Safety Town, he stepped forward, and said words I will never forget. "In my entire life, no one has ever said 'I am proud of you, Mike,' until this lady gave me a chance. When you little kids turn the corners in *Safety Town*, I want you to know someone else has turned a corner, and that's me!"

After the ribbon-cutting, Mike shared that he had completed his community service hours long before he finished *Safety Town* and planned to head to Florida where his sister was going to help him find a job. We named the church after Mike. Faith was such an integral part of what we accomplished. I often wonder about the rest of Mike's story.

Grounded in Mike's story is the advice I passed along to our grandson, Tom, at his school's Grandparent's Day when he was in 7th grade...."everyone has a story, look beyond what you first see and listen to as many stories as you can."

Letter to My Younger Self

HEY, SLOW DOWN! Please note, that racing through life at high speed is a lot like a roll of toilet paper! Yep, the closer you get to the end of the roll, the faster it goes! Take a few moments from rolling along in a busy schedule to recall "stoking the furnace," a sweaty household chore when I was young. "Stoking" required cranking the metal handle to open the furnace chamber, shoveling in coal and poking an iron rod inside to stir up flames and create more efficient burn. The relevance of being tasked with a "stoker" chore, early in life, leads me to " cranking up" memories of myself as the passage of time accelerates.

As an inquisitive five-year-old, I was already "stoking" a burning desire to learn. I jumped on the yellow school bus with my one-year older brother who was starting First Grade in a one-room school house. Since Kindergarten was not available and Mrs. Hunter didn't object, I poked my way enthusiastically into the first of 23 years of formal schooling, and loved every minute of reading, writing, math, science and social studies. Art and physical education, not so much! The flames of learning sparked a career ultimately including 45 years of teaching, leadership, and continued education. Four and one-half decades would eventually be filled with gratifying experiences in Home Economics, Adult Education, Community Education, Media Services, Community and Business Partnerships and Early Childhood Education and Services. The transitions from one to another are already reduced to embers, but persistence in "stoking" the ashes and trusting God's wisdom led me to an administrative role, championing school readiness for thousands of Birth—5 year olds.

The flames continued to crackle as I jumped into partnerships that, in turn, "stoked" the fires of school and operational levies, efforts to build strong families, restoration of a crumbling historical theater, addressing residential and personal needs of off-track teens, fundraising through partnerships with the St. Cloud Area Chamber of Commerce, the Brian Klinefelter Foundation, the Community Foundation, St. Cloud Arts Council, Catholic Charities, St. Paul's Church and local schools. Sighs of satisfaction are rekindled when I notice the ISD 742 logo being refreshed at today's schools or I visit the beautifully restored Paramount Theater, celebrating in 2021, its 100th Anniversary.

Rolling past retirement, I savor gratifying memories of hundreds of dedicated, kind, talented women and men with whom I worked. Even a post-retirement tragedy does not extinguish my view of work. A lightening-induced fire destroyed all of the resources, records and classrooms in the old, old building where young children were championed. Memories and accomplishments of children and their teachers will never be extinguished.

I remember the day when the furnace "stoker" box arrived at our home. Transferring the coal into the furnace became automatic, once the coal was shoveled into the stoker machine. So too, my roles as "stoker" faded with retirement. Through the words of Hopi Indian Chief White Eagle, I ponder the future of our world. Chief White Eagle predicts a time when we will be required to chose between a "door or a hole." The decision to fall into the hole or go through the door belongs to each of us. Consuming information 24 hours a day, with negative energy, nervousness and pessimism, will result in falling into the hole. But, taking the opportunity to look at oneself, rethinking life and death, taking care of ourselves and others, can guide us through the "door" of resilience. Chief White Eagle reminds us to assume an Eagle's perspective, seeing everything from above with a broader vision.

The design of my future calls for commitment. Will I be a "stoker" of kindness, service and peace, fueling harmony in relationships, human endeavors and unity, or will I fall in a hole? Today's furnace "stoking" no longer requires messy coal. "Stoking" love, equality, and selflessness will likewise require a different energy, keeping the blaze of man and womankind ignited with purpose and meaning.

Toilet paper has become another matter. Is it possible that our future could be threatened by coming to the end of the roll before we have finished our business?

Giving Thanks

AS THE BIG day for noodles, family gatherings and hitting the "turkey button" draws close, I am thinking about gratitude and all the things I could jot on my "I Am Thankful" list! November, 2018 finds Garry and I driving to Arizona and then on to Yorba Linda, CA to join Andrea, Sean, Izzy, Eli, Ethan and Poppy to enjoy a family Thanksgiving! If all goes well, more family will join us.

At the top of my thankful list is "Everything FAMILY!" There are simply no words for the immeasurable gratitude for my parents, husband, children, grandchildren, siblings, nieces, nephews, cousins, uncles and aunts (including all "in-laws"). It doesn't matter if that love is beamed to Heaven or across the room, over many miles or "through the cloud" of technology...family is #1!

Setting family securely in the joy of my heart, where do I start with gratitude? Ann Voskamp, in her book, One Thousand Gifts, has a thought. Voskamp, author, every-day mother of 6 children, wife of a farmer and witness to her 3 year old sister's accidental death, has written an inspirational book searching for "grounding" in her 'where is God' life. After years of uncertainty, fear and inner turmoil, she slowly gathers an understanding of the power of "thanks giving" for EVERYTHING. In turn, understanding illuminates not only God's gifts of remarkable joy, but also those gifts sent to repair our "soul holes."

Voskamp gives meaning to the concept of gratitude through the words of Sarah Ban Breathnach with this meaningful quote...*Gratitude bestows reverence, allowing us to encounter everyday epiphanies, those transcendent moments of awe that change forever how we experience life and the world.* Voskamp's friend challenges her to simply make a list of 1,000 things that she loves...1,000 blessings of sorts...the tiny things! The rest of her story highlights Voskamp's journey as she moves to heal her life's wounds through faith and discovery of the secret to "living joy" in every situation, whether hands are full or empty.

So, here we go....I started my list and invite you to keep a little notebook somewhere handy and create your own. Here is the beginning of mine...

1. Goose bumps (I have no idea why that popped into my mind first...I know I have more to say about goose bump moments in my life)
2. "In-the-moment" photo or text sending the message... "I am thinking about you!"
3. Red, yellow, orange leaves in the fall
4. A friend's name appearing in the caller ID box or the e-mail address box
5. Enthusiastic leaf-flapping of the solar-powered plastic daisy (drenched in sunshine) on my windowsill

And so, the list of little things (which are abundantly sprinkled among the BIG things) in my little notebook will continue.....

I have mixed emotions about the fact that so many retail stores are open on Thanksgiving, but take heart in the fact that several stores have reversed the trend and will allow their employees to be home with their families! Meanwhile, the important stuff will be a priority in our house...the aromas of turkey baking and noodles simmering is in order and signs for continuing these traditions into the next generation are looking good.

more gifts on the list.....

6. Remembering Mom making homemade noodles with great-grandchildren

7. Egg shells to measure cream for the noodles
8. Cream pie with real whipping cream, real butter, real vanilla and real sugar
9. Homemade rolls from Mom's recipe for "Sunday Rolls"
10. Grammas, moms, daughters, kids, grandkids and great grandkids creating yummy goodies!

Isabella and Lucia

I can't think of anything Mom enjoyed more than passing along the recipes and traditions that created memories during the holidays. From her heavenly vantage point, she is surely loving the fact that flour continues to "fly" everywhere! Ever conscious of healthy eating, I tried noodles with gluten-free flour. It did not make the list of "1,000 Gifts!" So grateful for the memories yesterday...and those to come!

My heart trusts in Him, and He helps me.
My heart leaps for joy, and with my song I praise Him.
Psalm 28:7

I'm Gonna' Climb that Mountain

AS INTERSTATE 70 motorists pass through Albuquerque, New Mexico, they drive under an amazing multi-level, mountainous highway structure that takes drivers north, south, east, west and every direction in between. Drivers can select destinations and exit to places such as Las Cruces, Santa Fe, Oklahoma City or Surprise, Arizona. I love this dusty pink concrete spider web; it is a masterpiece of engineering technology, aesthetically and creatively pleasing to the eye, a monument of organizational genius and a remarkable testimony to directional efficiency and functionality.

If I were sitting on top of this awesome structure contemplating the destination of thousands of vehicles each day, I might think of these multiple roads as an analogy for life…..there are so many different possibilities for destinations….so, I wonder, does one choose destinations or are destinations placed in our paths by a higher power, who has a plan for us. It seems as though my own personal journey just kind of happened, with some very special highlights…..and now I arrive at this last quarter of my life and wonder "what's it all about?" I certainly don't welcome descriptive labels of "senior, silver, senile, over-the-hill…"

New York Times commentator, David Brooks, in a thought-provoking book titled The Second Mountain, separates life's climb as two separate mountains. In climbing the first mountain, humans define success goals including desires to be well thought of, to get invited into the right groups and to experience personal happiness, along with all the stuff our culture endorses such as a nice home, close family, fun vacations, good food and great friends. On the first mountain, not unlike choosing a particular route through the mountainous Albuquerque bridge, a person makes individual choices and chooses one or more directional options.

Nearly thirty years ago, my son gave me a book that influenced much of my professional career as teacher, community educator and administrative leader. The "success" literature at the time tied character ethics, like integrity, courage, justice, patience, etc. to the personality ethic, including personality traits, skills, techniques and maintaining a positive attitude. Steven Covey compiled two centuries of success literature in his best selling "The 7 Habits of Highly Effective People," shifting emphasis from practices to principles using an "inside-out" approach to starting change within oneself. Covey's seven habits are designed to move us through dependence to independence (Mountain 1) to interdependence (Mountain 2).

Covey focuses first on being proactive, beginning with the end in mind and putting first things first. Brooks suggests that once humans reach the top of the first mountain, there may often be a question, "now what," wondering if the human spirit doesn't have a deeper quest. On the second mountain we are more comfortable with win/win, seeking first to understand before being understood and to pull aspects of life together by synergization. Something, perhaps divine, as we age, calls us to make a commitment, tie oneself down and give ourselves away without expectation of return.

Two years ago, just as I was feeling the uncertainties of my "older stage," I hoped David's perspective would guide my own search for commitment to others. "Out of the blue," a global pandemic of the Covid 19 Virus swept the world paralyzing every aspect of life. As of this writing, most of the world has experienced some level of quarantine during the past two years, with hardly a glimmer of hope for total recovery. The world is changing after many months of devastation, unbelievable death tolls, postponement of milestones and celebrations, the race to a cure, economic devastation, workplaces redefined and education a "whole new ballgame." A return to normalcy becomes more uncertain. Thousands of Americans and global humanity adjust our dress, behaviors and attitudes in spite of a more treacherous Mountain One. The harsh reality of survival during the pandemic forces many to turn their lives and livelihoods upside down in their commitment to the well-being of others.

The Covid 19 Pandemic brought medical and care professionals to the forefront of respect, gratitude and heroism. Young children donated birthday money or held fundraisers to buy food and toilet paper for those who were sick, isolated or hungry. Sir Thomas Moore, a 100 year old World War II veteran, challenged himself to push his walker 100 laps around his home. Sir Thomas raised more than 18 million dollars bringing food, medicine, safety and love to fellow human beings before his own death from Covid 19. As of the last week in November, 2021, there have been 260,088,761 Covid cases, with 5,197,052 deaths, recorded on the Coronavirus-Worldometer. Both Delta and Omicron variants have begun their intrusion into a fading "normalcy."

The Pandemic has already and will continue to bring change. It will take the world's best efforts to create solutions and preventative measures for these deadly viruses. Today, our world is immersed in these efforts, suggesting that Stephen Covey's 7th Habit, "Sharpen the Saw," will never be outdated. Most efforts will be initiated on Mountain 1, as we build capacity and protection for all of humanity. Political intervention and a weary humanity have everyone clamoring for footholds in their quest for stability, faith and a return to joyful living.

There has never been a more critical time to fall in love with something—a person or a cause or an idea and if that love is deep enough, dedication of a signifiant chunk of effort will follow. Brooks writes that "the soul yearns for the fusion of righteousness and good," and opportunities abound on Mountain 2. The humanness that we so desperately miss, will return when each of us shares the reconstruction of mental, social/emotional and spiritual dimensions in a shared quest for joy.

Collaborative efforts of Tibet's Dalai Lama and Archbishop Desmond Tutu offer more Mountain 2 messages within the original twelfth-century Buddhist tradition. Jojong text echoes the Dalai Lama and Archbishop's beliefs that experiencing joy requires "looking away from oneself." Further, all dharma teachings of mind-training, agree on one point — the importance of "lessening one's self-absorption."

I have no doubt that God has had a plan for me all along. The further down the road I travel, the closer I am to understanding that real success and a life worth living, is not necessarily climbing higher in any aspect of life. It starts with acknowledgment that God loves everyone unconditionally. True success and subsequent joy come from being a good steward of the abilities and resources in one's life, with which God has blessed each of us.

Singing group, Alabama, offers further inspiration with this lyric from **Mountain Music**—*"I'm gonna climb that mountain!"* Don't fence me in! In Psalms 121:1-2 it is proclaimed, *I lift my eyes to the mountains—where does my help come from? My help comes from the LORD, the Maker of heaven and earth. I am ready to proceed! Father, may I?*

Epilogue

Look Both Ways

I started recording my memories with the intention of preserving some of our family history for our grandchildren. I found myself growing both in spiritual self-awareness and appreciation for so much beyond my "little world." As I pause at the end of memories to date in December, 2021, the world continues its struggle with challenges of the Covid-19 pandemic. I hope each reader will find resilience and encouragement in getting to the other side of fear, anger and isolation.

As our own country becomes more divisive, the lesson of "LOOK BOTH WAYS….becomes critically important!" That simple lesson may well save American democracy and restore freedoms, selflessness, motivation, equality, generosity, connectedness and affection in what's left of the 21st Century. Critical reminders to look both ways caution us….

- to accept and ponder that there are two sides to every story…. or three or sixteen;
- to consider the implications of feeling "left behind" or "right on;
- to remain discerning and thoughtful in merging "right" or "left" and
- to search for the truth before believing and to understand before accepting

FATHER, MAY I...

Before we cross the road to anger, dislike, or hatred, the age-old chicken question suggests more options of "both ways" considerations.
Why did the chicken cross the street?

… because she had her feathers ruffled on her side of the street; or
… he was too chicken to express his opinion on his own side of the issue; or
… because she sought grains of wisdom on the other side; or
… he sought kernels of truth

So, I leave the answer to our Savior,
There is no question that Jesus looked both ways before he crossed the desert, messaging…
"love one another as I have loved you"

CPSIA information can be obtained
at www.ICGtesting.com
Printed in the USA
BVHW081142030522
635994BV00029B/837